THE ANCIEN REGIME

William Doyle

MACMILLAN

First published 1986

Published by
MACMILLAN EDUCATION LTD
Houndmills, Basingstoke, Hampshire RG21 2XS
and London
Companies and representatives
throughout the world

Printed in Great Britain by
Anchor Brendon Ltd, Tiptree, Essex

British Library Cataloguing in Publication Data
Doyle, William
The Ancien Regime.—(Studies in European history)
1. France—History—Bourbons, 1589–1789—
Historiography
I. Title   II. Series
044'.03'072   DC121.3
ISBN 0–333–38696–5

Series Standing Order

If you would like to receive future titles in this series as they are
published, you can make use of our standing order facility. To place a
standing order please contact your bookseller or, in case of difficulty,
write to us at the address below with your name and address and the
name of the series. Please state with which title you wish to begin your
standing order. (If you live outside the United Kingdom we may not
have the rights for your area, in which case we will forward your order
to the publisher concerned.)

Customer Services Department, Macmillan Distribution Ltd
Houndmills, Basingstoke, Hampshire, RG21 2XS, England.

THE ANCIEN REGIME

Studies in European History

General Editor: Richard Overy
Editorial Consultants: John Breuilly
Roy Porter

PUBLISHED TITLES

William Doyle, The Ancien Regime
R. W. Scribner, The German Reformation
R. J. Service, The Russian Revolution

FORTHCOMING

T. C. W. Blanning, The French Revolution
Peter Burke, The Renaissance
Michael Dockrill, The Cold War 1945–1963
Geoffrey Ellis, The Napoleonic Empire
R. J. Geary, Labour Politics 1900–1930
Mark Greengrass, Calvinism in Early Modern Europe, *c.* 1560–1685
Henry Kamen, Golden Age Spain
Richard MacKenney, The City State and Urban Liberties, *c.* 1450–
1650
Roger Price, The Revolutions of 1848
Geoffrey Scarre, Witchcraft and Magic in 16th and 17th Century
Europe
Clive Trebilcock, Problems in European Industrialisation 1800–1914

Contents

In memory of John Bromley

Editor's Preface

The main purpose of this new series of Macmillan studies is to make available to teacher and student alike developments in a field of history that has become increasingly specialised with the sheer volume of new research and literature now produced. These studies are designed to present the 'state of the debate' on important themes and episodes in European history since the sixteenth century, presented in a clear and critical way by someone who is closely concerned himself with the debate in question.

The studies are not intended to be read as extended bibliographical essays, though each will contain a detailed guide to further reading which will lead students and the general reader quickly to key publications. Each book carries its own interpretation and conclusions, while locating the discussion firmly in the centre of the current issues as historians see them. It is intended that the series will introduce students to historical approaches which are in some cases very new and which, in the normal course of things, would take many years to filter down into the textbooks and school histories. I hope it will demonstrate some of the excitement historians, like scientists, feel as they work away in the vanguard of their subject.

The format of the series conforms closely with that of the companion volumes of studies in economic and social history which has already established a major reputation since its inception in 1968. Both series have an important contribution to make in publicising what it is that historians are doing and in making history more open and accessible. It is vital for history to communicate if it is to survive.

R. J. OVERY

A Note on References

References are cited throughout in brackets according to the numbering in the general bibliography, with page references where necessary indicated by a colon after the bibliography number.

Preface

The aim of this essay is neither to chronicle the Ancien Regime nor to analyse it. It is to describe and discuss the way the Ancien Regime has been thought and written about since the French revolutionaries first coined the term. In their eyes its meaning was self-evident. Subsequent debate and discussion, however, has expanded that meaning far beyond anything its originators dreamed of, so that the idea of the Ancien Regime has become extremely elastic. Historians have disagreed, often radically, about what it was, where it operated, how it worked, when it began, and when it ended. Students are often unaware of the range of questions they may be begging whenever they use this apparently straightforward term. What follows is an attempt to guide them through this hitherto uncharted intellectual minefield: to explain how the concept of the Ancien Regime originated and developed down to our own century, and why historians continue to find it a fruitful, though problematical, framework for thinking about pre-modern times.

1   Evolution of an Idea 1789–1914

The Ancien Regime was created by the French Revolution. It was what the revolutionaries thought they were destroying in and after 1789. Nobody before that momentous year thought of themselves as living under something called the Ancien Regime. *Ancien* means not so much 'old' as 'former'; and there can be no former regime until there is a new one.

Historians disagree about when the old order ended and the new one began. Contemporaries too were uncertain. The first use of the term *Ancien Régime* appears to have been made in 1788, by a noble pamphleteer anticipating the glories of a new regime to be built around the Estates-General. The elections to this body in the spring of 1789 seemed firm evidence that the new dawn was indeed breaking, and some clerical electors were found referring to the conditions they had hitherto lived under as the 'former regime'. Once the Estates-General had met, transmuted itself into the National Constituent Assembly, and survived its first crises in July and October 1789, the deputies began to refer regularly in their speeches and decrees to the 'preceding' regime, or simply the old (*vieux*) one [40:*10–16*]. By early 1790, however, Ancien Regime had become the standard term for what had obtained before the Revolution. By 1792 the term 'ancient regime', a direct if none-too-accurate translation, was being used in English to describe the same thing.

(i) Initial Definitions

What sort of regime did the men of 1789 think they were replacing? It is clear that when they first used this new term they had in mind two different, though interconnected, things.

The first meaning was political. The Ancien Regime had been a system of government. Many dictionaries treat this as a sufficient definition even today. The fundamental characteristics of Ancien Regime government, the revolutionaries thought, were that the king ruled by arbitrary power, and without representative institutions. Under the absolute monarchy brought to a peak of refinement in the later seventeenth-century by Louis XIV – and little had changed since – all sovereignty, all authority and all power were concentrated in the person of the king; and he was answerable for their exercise to nobody but God. Under such a government, the men of 1789 believed, nobody had any rights, no person or property was secure, and no agreed rules or laws bound the conduct of public affairs. Men remembered how, in November 1787, Louis XVI caught off-guard had declared that what was legal was what he wished. Most still believed in 1789 that the despotic tendencies of the old government sprang more from the unbridled ambitions of the king's advisers, ministers and agents, than from the monarch's own inclinations. But there was little consolation in that. During the political struggles and debates which culminated in the collapse of the old government in the summer of 1788, men began to talk about the need for a constitution to regulate all these matters on a permanent basis. They were aware that at that very moment the Americans were elaborating just such a document. And on 7 July 1789, even before the fall of the Bastille, the newly-established National Assembly declared itself a constituent (or constitution-making) body. The constitution it eventually produced in September 1791 was intended to embody the opposite of all that the Ancien Regime had been. It enshrined the sovereignty of the Nation; the rule of law; separation of powers; elective, representative government, and a wide range of guaranteed individual rights.

But this negative image of the Ancien Regime was not simply a set of political principles. From the very start the French Revolution had been concerned with social questions as well. Just two months after the Estates-General had first met, in the famous session on the night of 4 August, the deputies overthrew a whole range of basic social and economic institutions. These abolitions, together with a number of others which followed in the course of 1790 and 1791, were regarded as so fundamental that they too were embodied in

2

the constitution. The National Assembly, the preamble declared:

> abolishes irrevocably the institutions which wounded liberty and equality of rights.
>
> There is no longer either a nobility or a peerage, or hereditary distinctions, or distinctions of orders, or a feudal regime, or private justice, or any of the titles denominations or perogatives deriving from them, or any order of chivalry, or any of the corporations or decorations for which proofs of nobility were required, or which implied distinctions of birth, or any other superiority but that of public officials in the exercise of their duties.
>
> There is no longer venality or heredity of public office.
>
> There is no longer for any part of the nation or for any individual, any privilege or exception to the common law of all Frenchmen.
>
> There are no longer either guilds, or corporations of professions, arts and crafts.
>
> The law no longer recognises either religious vows or any other engagement contrary to natural rights or the constitution.

So the Ancien Regime was also a form of society. It had been dominated by the 'privileged orders' of clergy and nobility, who had been exempt from many common burdens but who had monopolised all public power and profits. Privileged, self-perpetuating oligarchies, in fact, had made the whole of pre-revolutionary society a chaotic, irrational jungle of special cases, exceptions and inequalities. By early 1790 another term was in widespread use to describe all this: aristocracy. And the most glaringly irrational manifestation of aristocracy had been feudalism, or 'the feudal regime', that system under which lords who did not own the land could levy dues on and exact obligations from people who did. For that majority of Frenchmen who were peasants, the disappearance of feudalism was perhaps the most basic of the changes that marked off the old regime from the new – although the 'time of the lords' would linger on in folk memory down to the early twentieth century [40:*17*].

3

The ideology of the French Revolution did not emerge all of a piece. It developed and refined itself with the movement of events. And so did the revolutionaries' concept of the Ancien Regime. The most momentous development to occur after the initial changes of 1789 was the quarrel with the Catholic Church which came into the open with the ill-fated oath of loyalty imposed on the clergy in November 1790. There had been little anti-religious feeling in 1789, but a good deal of anti-clericalism. This had manifested itself in the abolition of tithes, the confiscation and resale of church property, the abolition of monasticism and finally the attempt to reorganise the French church completely in the Civil Constitution of the Clergy. Many clergy also regarded the introduction of toleration for Protestants as an attack on the church. Whether or not that was the intention, the ecclesiastical policy of the Constituent Assembly certainly constituted a repudiation of an Ancien Regime in which a well-endowed and noble-controlled Catholic Church had enjoyed a monopoly of public worship and dominated the provision of both education and poor relief. That repudiation grew more determined after many clergy refused the oath of 1790 and the Pope finally denounced the Revolution. By 1794 many parts of France had been swept by a movement of 'dechristianisation', and the state was renouncing all religious affiliations. Even revolutionaries who deplored such extremes now regarded the Ancien Regime as a time of superstition and fanaticism. Clearly, then, here was a third meaning: the Ancien Regime was a religious and spiritual as well as a political and social order.

The attack on established religion made the Revolution more than just a French affair. The Roman Catholic Church was an international body, and an onslaught against it on this scale could not fail to have international repercussions. The revolutionaries' initial impulse had been to live at peace with the outside world, and to renounce the use of force in international relations. Foreign governments for their part were mostly well content to stand back and watch France wallowing in helpless chaos. But the very act of rationalising the country brought revolutionaries into conflict with foreign authorities, some of whom enjoyed sovereign rights over enclaves within France. The Pope was one, at Avignon, and a successful request by his subjects there to be incorporated into France complicated his relations with the new regime even further. German princes also enjoyed rights in Alsace which were challenged by France's new doctrines of national sovereignty. After Louis XVI's abortive attempt to emigrate in June 1791, foreign monarchs began to take a more serious interest in his fate, and when the Emperor and the King of Prussia made clear their concern in the declaration of Pillnitz (August 1791) and gave open hospitality to aristocratic French *émigrés*, it became increasingly apparent that the Ancien Regime might yet be restored through foreign machinations. France went to war in April 1792 to prevent this, and the first result of the war was to bring down the monarchy. When, therefore, the French armies finally took the offensive that autumn, they did so in the name of a republic, and against monarchs and all the institutions that supported them. By offering 'fraternity and help to all peoples who wish to recover their liberty' they invited subjects to revolt everywhere. With the slogan 'War on the castles, peace to the cottages' they identified themselves with social revolutions wherever they went. In December, French generals were instructed to set up new authorities in occupied territories and see to the election of persons 'faithful to liberty and equality, and who renounce privileges'. Feudalism was to be destroyed, and church lands confiscated. In other words, the Ancien Regime was now regarded not merely as a French phenomenon. It could be found wherever there were kings, nobles, privileges, feudalism and ecclesiastical property. And that meant most of Europe.

(ii) The polarisation of opinion

Historical objectivity played no part in the initial definition of the Ancien Regime. The revolutionaries defined it in order to condemn it. This set a pattern for much subsequent discussion of it as a historical phenomenon even among serious scholars. What they thought of the Ancien Regime very much depended on what they thought of the Revolution. The first instinct of uninformed onlookers, and even informed ones, was to assume that the elected representatives of the French Nation knew what they were talking about. If they condemned and rejected the Ancien Regime so vehemently, it must surely have deserved it, and been what they said. And so at first the revolutionaries' picture of the government, society and church they were dismantling won wide acceptance. Even Arthur Young, the English traveller who had seen more of the Ancien Regime in its death-throes than most, accepted in 1791 that 'it will scarcely be attempted to be urged that a revolution was not absolutely necessary for the welfare of the kingdom'. Within a few years, however, he was to modify his opinion quite radically. By then, extremes had been reached which no previous oppression seemed to justify. Besides, by then too the Ancien Regime had begun to find defenders.

The first, and greatest, was Edmund Burke. His *Reflections on the Revolution in France* (1790) was mainly an indignant rebuttal of the idea that English liberty and the liberty proclaimed by the French Revolution had anything in common. Whereas the English had built upon their inherited institutions, the French had repudiated theirs wholesale, and so their reforms were without roots. They would have done better to modify and amend the Ancien Regime, in which they 'had the elements of a constitution very nearly as good as could be wished'. It was true that it lacked the representative institutions of England, but those could have been introduced without the upheavals that actually occurred. Despite all its abuses, the old monarchy had been 'a despotism rather in appearance than in reality' and had shown itself if anything too willing to countenance reform under Louis XVI.

The privileges enjoyed by the nobility and clergy had been much exaggerated, their conduct had been honorable and civilised, and marked by no 'incorrigible vices'. In any case: 'To be honoured and even privileged by the laws, opinions and inveterate usages of our country, growing out of the prejudice of ages, has nothing to provoke horror and indignation in any man'. Above all, Burke was scandalised by the attack on the church, which was in fact only beginning as he wrote. Established religion, complete with all its independent endowments, was in his view one of the foundations of any well-balanced society: 'We know, and what is better, we feel inwardly, that religion is the basis of civil society, and the source of all good and of all comfort'.

What this meant was that the Revolution had demolished a state, a society and a religious establishment that were fundamentally healthy and sound: in need of reform perhaps, but not of destruction. This confronted Burke with the problem of why in that case there had been a revolution. His answer was one that was to echo down the historiography of the Ancien Regime to our own day. There had been a conspiracy. The minds of Frenchmen had been corrupted by the writings of a 'literary cabal' which 'had some years ago formed something like a regular plan for the destruction of the Christian religion'. These writers had allied with a 'monied interest' of rootless plutocrats who looked with greed on the vast estates of the church, and with envy on the social prestige of the nobility, to bring down and plunder the precious heritage of centuries of French historical development. Variants of the conspiracy theory of the French Revolution also proliferated throughout the 1790s in France, Germany, Scotland and elsewhere [16], but few of their proponents spent much time in discussing the nature of the Ancien Regime. They took its virtues for granted as self-evident, for unlike Burke in 1790 they were largely addressing themselves to an audience that had made up its mind. The revolution stood for plunder, violence, mindless bloodshed and chaos. It hardly needed to be emphasised that the Ancien Regime had been a time of tranquillity, order, subordination, respect for property and reverence for religion.

Yet this was to accept more of the revolutionaries' version of things than their detractors would have cared to admit. Both versions depended on the presumption that 1789 had marked a fundamental break in the history of France; that there was no continuity and nothing in common between what preceded the great upheaval and what followed. The most important of all the admirers of the Ancien Regime, Napoleon himself, certainly took that view. This was why his rule was marked by a resolute attempt to bring back the salient features of pre-revolutionary times – church, monarchy, court and nobility. His aim was quite consciously to reconcile the old France and the new. This policy was highly controversial, but it did not advance historical debate about the Ancien Regime. Debate of any sort was muted under Napoleon. It was not until after 1815 that the stereotypes of the 1790s began to be modified.

Even now the main concern was with the Revolution, and discussion of the Ancien Regime remained a by-product. Although the Bourbons could not have been restored without accepting much of what had been done since 1789, neither they nor the *émigrés* who returned with them felt constrained to like it. Nor did they make any secret of their fundamental preference for the Ancien Regime. After all, they derived their own claims to legitimacy and their social, political and spiritual models from those times. In this hostile atmosphere, adherents of the revolutionary legacy felt defensive, and for the first time they began to argue that the Revolution had been as much part of French traditions as a repudiation of them [11]. While monarchists extolled the powers of the restored king's ancestors, aristocrats the exploits of the forebears of the returned *émigrés*, and clericals the Christian authority of the old Gallican Church, liberals argued that liberty was not new to France in 1789. A tradition of freedom ran right back into the Frankish mists, and the Revolution had merely reasserted it after a century and a half of royal despotism, aristocratic tyranny and clerical fanaticism. The implication was that the Ancien Regime was not something immobile and unchanging. It had developed, however undesirably, and so far from being calm, ordered and deferential, its history was tumultuous and full of conflicts quite as spectacular or horrific as those of the Revolution. Even if blown off course into excesses few cared to defend, the Revolution had been a sincere attempt to restore and safeguard France's tradition of freedom by endowing the nation with a constitution. To which some conservatives replied that it was absurd to claim that there had been no constitution under the Ancien Regime. The achievements of the pre-revolutionary state were proof to the contrary.

In all this lay the seeds of a more sophisticated assessment of the Ancien Regime as a historical phenomenon. Not all of them germinated at once, and indeed they would need to be fertilised by new research before they did. Few of those who discussed these subjects between the restoration and the 1848 revolution did much original research, especially on the Ancien Regime. It was after all merely the overture to their real preoccupation. The exception was Joseph Droz [10], who in 1839 began to produce the first serious analysis of the fall of the old order. It is true that the aim was still polemical: Droz wished to refute the most popular contemporary celebration of the Revolution's inevitability, that by François Mignet [9]. His basic argument was to become a classic: that the Revolution could have been avoided if the selfish and shortsighted privileged orders had rallied behind a reforming monarch rather than obstructing his plans. Droz's book was the fruit of 28 years of thought and reading, remarkably detailed and well informed, and sober in judgement. Its impact was unfortunately muted amid a general revival of enthusiasm for the revolutionary tradition which marked the last uninspiring years of the July monarchy. The romantic yearnings which made Michelet's or Louis Blanc's histories of the Revolution such best sellers found no appeal in the Ancien Regime, one of 'those decadent ages in which no Ideal either grows or blossoms' (Carlyle). It was only after 1848, when revolution had once again been tried, and once again gone wrong, that the virtues of more sober analysis recovered some of their attraction.

(iii) Towards scholarly analysis

Serious scholarly study of the Ancien Regime began in 1856. This was the year of publication of Alexis de Tocqueville's *L'Ancien Régime et la Révolution Française*. Not that the aim of this disillusioned liberal politician was fundamentally scholarly. He wrote to understand not the past, but his own times. Yet that in itself involved understanding the past better, and to do so Tocqueville went beyond the memoirs and revolutionary polemics hitherto forming the main sources for the history of the Ancien Regime. He went to the archives, and provincial ones at that. It is true that he spent only a few months there, and that what he found largely confirmed and served to flesh out ideas whose outlines had been in his mind for two decades [1, 3]. Nevertheless he showed the way to untapped riches that historians are still mining. Tocqueville went beyond the restoration liberal historians in minimising the break of 1789. For him the Revolution merely strengthened and completed a number of long-term underlying trends in French society. The inevitable drift of modern history, he thought, was towards equality. The danger was that it would open the way to despotism and the destruction of liberty. This danger had been immeasurably increased by the Revolution which, so far from establishing liberty, had swept away most of the institutions through which it functioned, and thereby opened the way to the unchecked despotism of Napoleon. The centralisation for which Tocqueville and his liberal contemporaries blamed many of the ills of nineteenth-century France was in fact nothing new. It had been a basic feature of the Ancien Regime. Equally basic, however, had been the obstacles in its way, vestiges of the once fuller liberty of the middle ages, in the form of privileges, immunities, prescriptive rights and independent institutions such as the clergy and the lawcourts. Despotism had never entirely succeeded in eliminating them. That was the historic task of the Revolution, whose driving force, the impulse to equality, was that of History itself.

This interpretation, though unashamedly a tract for Tocqueville's own times, implied that the Ancien Regime was something to be understood rather than attacked or defended. It was a subject worthy of study in its own right; for after all men had lived under recognisably the same organisation of the state and society for several centuries before 1789, and the tides of history were flowing just as strongly, if less spectacularly, during that time as in the 1790s. For Tocqueville the Ancien Regime was the middle ages in ruins. Nor was it peculiar to France. Most of Europe had exactly the same institutions, the remnants of what he located in the fourteenth century as 'the old constitution of Europe' [18:*ch.4*]. Much of the book was devoted to investigating why, if European institutions were so uniform, the revolution that was to destroy them finally, and level the ruins, occurred first in France. This enquiry led Tocqueville into areas of investigation little touched by his predecessors, but which have been the central preoccupations of subsequent historians. He was the first to analyse how Ancien Regime government actually worked outside the corridors of Versailles. He was the first to look behind the picture of French society and institutions drawn by the men of 1789, and to ask how far it was accurate. He was the first too to draw attention to the economic character of the old order which, he argued, ended in a blaze of prosperity. His account of all these things has been much amended and modified by subsequent research, but not his estimate of their importance. Yet his final answer to the question which had led him to broach them drew him back to his original, grander preoccupations. The overthrow of the Ancien Regime began in France because there centralised government had excluded everybody from all say in or experience of public affairs, and thereby deprived men of all sense of public duty. In these circumstances they were seduced by the impractical dreams of the Enlightenment, which gave them a fatal contempt for existing institutions. Tocqueville's pioneering analysis thus ended curiously close to the Burkean idea that the Revolution was the result of a philosophic plot.

Conspiracy theories had an obvious appeal to all who found something to admire in the Ancien Regime. For Tocqueville, it was the vestiges of former liberty. For Hyppolite Taine it was order, and the fruits of organic growth. Writing a generation later than Tocqueville, Taine was another disillusioned liberal. A supporter of the revolution of 1848 when young, he had grown increasingly hostile over the years to democratic ideas, and his distaste was confirmed by the excesses of the Commune of 1871. He came to history late, when his reputation as a literary critic and psychologist was already secure. The objective of *Les origines de la France contemporaine* (1875–93) was to seek to explain why France had given herself 13 constitutions in 80 years yet was still unsatisfied. Taine thought the answer lay in the reckless abandonment of the Ancien Regime in 1789, and his first, best and most celebrated volume was devoted to an analysis of that regime. Like Tocqueville, he went to the archives, and the book is dedicated to the archivists and librarians who had helped him. But he went to them for colour rather than for new information, since he knew basically what he thought before he started. Like Burke, whom he had encountered in his wide reading of English literature, he believed that every society has its own special character, the product of a unique evolution. That did not preclude further evolution, but to abandon the heritage of the past wholesale was to invite disaster and open the way to the sort of anarchy seen in France after 1789. Taine no more approved of the whole of the Ancien Regime than did Tocqueville. He could see that it contained many injustices, inequalities and inefficiencies. But it was a natural growth and it kept men in order; and these virtues outweighed all its defects. It could have gone on evolving; but in 1789 Frenchmen took the wrong turning, impelled to abandon their entire heritage under the leadership of an educated minority seduced by the 'classical spirit', the habit of thinking in abstract, rational categories represented by the Enlightenment. Reason taught them that everything could be changed and at once put to rights; but 'in history, it is better to go on than start again' [19:*35*] and the overthrow of the Ancien Regime merely released the manic energies of an uncultivated rabble determined to destroy all order and all property. The Ancien Regime, therefore, was perfectly viable, but subverted. Taine offered little new evidence in support of his views, unlike Tocqueville. But he expressed himself in brilliant style, and his denunciation of the Revolution appealed to all those who disliked the Third Republic at a time when republican politicians, not to mention historians, were seeking to bolster the regime's legitimacy by strident appeals to revolutionary traditions [12]. Taine was no Catholic, but his arguments appealed to upholders of the established church and opponents of its disestablishment. He was no monarchist either, but believers in restoration found comfort in the thought that monarchy was the natural form of government evolved on French soil. Later, when he was long dead, fascists, anti-communists and right-wing extremists would welcome his emphasis on order and authority and his contempt for the populace.

Tocqueville and Taine sired important traditions in the interpretation of the Ancien Regime which have deeply influenced historians down to our own day. There is also a third tradition, surprisingly late to establish itself, but nowadays perhaps the most influential of all. This is the economic interpretation, and it goes back to Marx. For Marx the fundamental development of modern history had been the replacement of the feudal mode of production by the capitalist mode. In social terms this meant that the bourgeoisie supplanted the old landed aristocracy at the helm of society. It was not a swift process, but it was punctuated by violent struggles whenever the bourgeoisie had accumulated enough economic power to take over political authority. The French Revolution was the supreme example of such struggles, when feudalism was finally uprooted in France after a bourgeois seizure of power. Something like this interpretation had occurred to one of the leading revolutionaries of 1789, Barnave, although it was not published until 1843, and made little enough impact then [21]. Tocqueville, as we have seen, touched on economic aspects of the Ancien Regime, but did not pursue them. It was left to Jean Jaurès, in his *Histoire Socialiste de la Révolution Française* (1901–4) to popularise the view that the old order's most important feature was its distinctive economic structure. It was the declining stage of feudalism, when the power of the old nobility was being sapped by other groups acquiring a share of the land, and more effective means of organising production were gaining strength through the progress of capitalism. Jaurès followed Tocqueville in emphasising the prosperity of the Ancien Regime's last years. That demonstrated the confidence of capitalism on the eve of its final triumph. But his attempt to stress economic factors made him aware of how ill-documented they were, and he founded a series for the publication of important economic documents relating to the Revolution.

Many of them, inevitably, were informative about the Ancien Regime as well, and they were to do much to sharpen the perspectives of twentieth-century historians writing about the pre-revolutionary age. Those perspectives are the subject of the rest of this study.

2 Anciens Regimes

The Ancien Regime was not a planned order of things. It had grown up slowly and haphazardly, by custom and habit. Laws were customary, rights were prescriptive. Powers, prerogatives and privileges endlessly overlapped and conflicted. The essence of the Ancien Regime, argues Pierre Goubert, was confusion [40: *22*]. In one sense, therefore, it defies rational analysis, just as the men of 1789 thought it defied rational reform. The only sensible course seemed to be to sweep away the whole edifice and begin again from first principles. The historian cannot brush it aside in this way. He has to grapple with its complexities and, even at the risk of distortion, find categories by which it can be better understood. None of them is entirely satisfactory or self-contained. All have given rise to wide-ranging historical debate and disagreement.

(i) Political

The men of 1789 thought they were overthrowing despotism. Tocqueville thought they were advancing it. Neither found much to admire or approve of in the Ancien Regime state. Later historians have been more divided, but unanimous at least in the view that it was not despotic.

The classic definition of despotism was formulated by Montesquieu in *De l'Esprit des Lois* of 1748. It was the rule of one man without laws. Monarchy properly so-called, on the other hand, was the rule of one man according to law. And to make sure he observed the law, in a monarchical state there were also certain 'intermediary bodies' placed between the ruler and the mass of his subjects, with the power to resist the one and protect the other. By these definitions the Ancien Regime state was not a despotism. The monarchy was certainly absolute, in the sense that no institution, group or individual had the right to resist the king's commands; and he had at his disposal a body of obedient, omnicompetent administrative agents in the provinces, the intendants, to enforce his will. But the king also observed and respected a vast range of laws and legal forms, and had to contend with a number of intermediary bodies. It is true that between 1614 and 1789 no national representative institution challenged monarchical power. But there were innumerable, quasi-independent, regional, local and sectional institutions, such as the clergy, the estates of certain provinces, municipalities, and countless companies and corporations enjoying legally sanctioned rights, liberties and privileges. All in some sense constrained the king's freedom of action. Above all there were the parlements, the sovereign courts of justice, which could delay royal legislation and criticise it in remonstrances. In this form, opposition was built into the state system, and conflict between crown and parlements was the principal theme of constitutional history between the sixteenth and the eighteenth centuries.

These were Tocqueville's medieval ruins, in which the spirit of liberty still flickered. Most French historians since his time, however, have taken a far less sympathetic view of their role. In their view, the monarchy before 1789 was the main force in French history for progress and modernisation, and those who impeded its work were privileged groups bent on nothing more than selfish obstruction. This interpretation emerged during the early years of the Third Republic. It lent legitimacy to France's pre-revolutionary history at a time when public orthodoxy was to glory in the achievements of the Revolution, by implying that the monarchy had been pursuing many of the same laudable ends: nation-building, rationalisation and the elimination of social privilege. 'One is struck above all', lamented Marcel Marion [25], the foremost authority on the Ancien Regime between the 1890s and the 1920s, 'by the ordinary powerlessness of central government to get itself obeyed, and in areas where only the drawbacks of despotism have been noticed, at least as apparent, above all in the eighteenth century, are the evils of a very real anarchy, and a general confusion amid which the last word did not lie...

with the sovereign.' The monarchy's great mistake, in Marion's view, was that it had not been despotic enough, and he made his reputation eulogising the strong ministers of the eighteenth century – Machault, Terray, Maupeou, Lamoignon – who vainly struggled to overcome the selfish opposition of the parlements.

Marion was a prolific scholar, and many of his works are still used by students of the Ancien Regime. And his general interpretation was eagerly adopted between the wars by adherents of *Action Française*, a monarchist movement with an obvious interest in evoking France's glorious achievements in times when kings ruled. Not all the numerous historians in sympathy with *Action Française* stressed the authoritarian potential of the monarchy. Frantz Funck-Brentano (who also acknowledged the influence of Taine) argued that the key institution of the Ancien Regime was the family, that the nation itself was one great family, and the king its patriarch [23]. His power,therefore, was benevolent. Even the *lettres de cachet*, those sealed orders under which kings could imprison anybody without trial, denounced by the revolutionaries as the most revolting symbol of despotism, were largely issued at the request of families wishing to discipline their more unruly members. So far from being a despot, the king was popular, accessible and responsive to public opinion. Other right-wing historians, impressed by Mussolini's Italian experiments with a corporate state, emphasised the corporative character of the Ancien Regime and its potential for harmony rather than conflict [63,73]. But the most popular of all the right-wingers, Pierre Gaxotte, maintained that the monarchy's fundamental historic mission was to destroy the institutions of opposition. In his eyes, the parlements were the mouthpiece of a reactionary nobility. The crown's traditional policy had been to ally with the progressive middle classes, the force of the future. If it had remained true to this alliance, the bourgeois revolution of 1789 would have been unnecessary. Louis XIV's strength had derived from a resolute anti-aristocratic policy, and even Louis XV had shown that monarchical vigour was not exhausted when, during his last years, he destroyed the power of the parlements. The greatest mistake Louis XVI ever made was to restore them [53].

Though a populariser rather than a scholar, Gaxotte has influenced writing on pre-revolutionary institutions down to the present day [45,57].In any case, his general interpretation is very close to that of a school of institutional historians tracing its intellectual ancestry to Georges Pagès. Pagès argued, at much the time Gaxotte was first writing, that the power of the Ancien Regime monarchy reached the peak of perfection in the early years of Louis XIV's personal rule, because it was then that the king's freedom of action was most untrammelled. Ever since medieval times the monarchy had been struggling to break out of the constraints imposed by feudal institutions.The wars of religion had shown the awful consequences of failing to do so, and for two-thirds of a century afterwards the monarchy strove to establish an authority that would banish the spectre of civil war forever. By the 1660s it had succeeded. The parlement of Paris had been silenced, and control of the provinces was assured by the installation of intendants. By these means 'the king and the state were now as one, and the royal will no longer met any obstacles it could not easily smash'[64]. Yet by the time Louis died, the monarchy had become 'deformed', in that it had become bureaucratised. The king had imprisoned himself in a vast administrative machine which now impeded rather than promoted necessary changes, and cut him and his successors off from the nation. The resulting isolation and atrophy led straight to the Revolution.

This was one of the monarchy's 'irreparable errors'. The other far antedated the rule of Louis XIV, but set insuperable limits to what he or monarchs before or after him could do: venality of offices. By selling public offices, and hereditary rights to them, on a massive scale the monarchy had raised vast sums in the sixteenth and early seventeenth centuries, and had won the attachment of the socially ambitious bourgeoisie who had bought them. But it had also lost control of its own servants, because the king was never able to buy the offices back by refunding the money. Venality, therefore, gave the magistrates of the parlements and all other courts independent tenure, and so made them enormously more formidable as obstacles to royal authority. This in turn had obliged the monarchy to set up a counter-bureaucracy of dismissable officials, the intendants. Antagonism between the venal *officiers* of the judiciary and the untenured *commissaires* of the administration was thus the driving force of constitutional conflict down to 1789.

These ideas and insights have been much elaborated by Pagès' most distinguished pupil, Roland Mousnier, who in turn has a whole school of disciples. Mousnier made his name with what is still the most detailed study available of the operation of venality [60]. Subsequently he explored and expounded the rules and procedures by which absolute monarchy worked. Mousnier's monarchy is an institution above and outside society, using its plenitude of power to guide, protect and mould the nation from a lofty perspective unavailable to any mere subject. Long historiographical tradition underlies this interpretation, but also unprecedentedly wide reading in seventeenth-century jurists and apologists for absolute monarchy [79]. To read Mousnier one would hardly realise that royal authority also had learned and perceptive critics[15]. But the tide of history was not flowing their way. They had chosen the wrong side in the 'three-hundred-year lawsuit' between *officiers* and *commissaires*, opting for 'continual, unintelligent and sterile opposition to all attempts at reform and progress made by the monarchy'. Kings like Louis XIV ('France's great revolutionary') overrode these obstacles, as did Louis XV in his last years. But Louis XVI surrendered to them, and so brought down the whole Ancien Regime.

Refurbished in this way, what is known in French history as the *thèse royale* continues to win wide acceptance [49]. Yet it has never gone entirely unchallenged. Ever since the late nineteenth century some historians of the parlements have argued that when in their remonstrances they accused the king of riding roughshod over established laws, customs and liberties, they were often correct [52,54,66]. Jean Egret, the foremost mid-twentieth-century authority on the sovereign courts, became steadily more sympathetic to their claims to be defenders of the nation against predatory governments [51]. And the American and British scholars who have invaded the French archives over the last 30 or 40 years are products of historiographical traditions which have always vaunted resistance to government. Not surprisingly, most of them have tended to take a more sceptical view of the claims, ambitions and achievements of absolute monarchy. They have drawn attention, for example, to the abundance of representative institutions at every level of government in late medieval France, and to the survival of many of them down to the early seventeenth century [59]. They have argued that the parlements were not always, or even normally, motivated by blind and narrow self-interest; that their interpretations of the law were often more soundly based than those adopted by the crown [68]; that they were never reduced to complete silence or subservience, even under Louis XIV [55]; and that their extra-judicial powers were not usurped, but an integral and essential part of the state apparatus rather than an obstacle to its smooth functioning [50]. Nor was it their resistance that finally brought the Ancien Regime down, but rather the inertia and incompetence of the government [43].

For the supposed efficiency and reformism of absolute monarchy has not escaped critical scrutiny either. Was it in reality ever anything but a constant search for new funds to pay for an over-ambitious foreign policy? The introduction of the intendants, those keystones of royal authority, is beginning to look increasingly like an *ad hoc* expedient designed to wring more money out of reluctant taxpayers [46]. They became permanent because they were successful. Successive attempts to make the nobility and the clergy pay more direct taxes, whether in the *capitation* of 1698 , the *dixième* of 1710, the *vingtième* of 1749 or the *subvention territoriale* of 1787 all came in time of war or its expensive aftermath. Only religion rivalled the weight of taxation as a motive for resisting the government, whether in outright popular rebellion in the seventeenth century, or constitutional obstruction from the parlements in the eighteenth. 'Absolutism', concludes Denis Richet [39], 'was, in great part, the child of taxation.' But the needs which prompted this taxation could also impede the progress of royal authority. Borrowing money through the sale of offices weakened the king's control over his own subordinates, while the constant need for stopgap finance until tax revenue came in produced a central financial administration where disorder was the norm. From the sixteenth century through to the eighteenth the state was constantly over-extended, and ministers staggered from one hand-to-mouth expedient to the next. There were repeated bankruptcies, and financiers whose resources and contacts held off collapse in one reign were ruthlessly persecuted in the next [47]. Keeping the monarchy afloat financially was a dangerous but lucrative private business which only the occasional minister ever thought of changing, and then usually to his cost [48]. And all policy-making, financial or otherwise, was the plaything of court factions; kings had only the most limited idea of what was happening outside the walls of Versailles.

None of this bears much resemblance to the lofty, efficient image of royal government presented by the tradition culminating with Mousnier. Even Louis XIV, the bureaucrat-king whom conscientious monarchs were to copy for over a century, looks less like a royal revolutionary than the prisoner of routines elaborated under the great cardinals who governed France between 1624 and 1661. His chief innovation was simply to take over the personal power that was lawfully his when he was old enough to do so. The rest was propaganda, although brilliant propaganda [65]. The magnificence of Versailles, the relentless public insistence on orthodoxy, uniformity and obedience, the serene confidence of classical art and culture, all overwhelmed contemporaries and many later observers – including historians. But it was a façade concealing a ramshackle reality of insubordination, resistance, lack of uniformity, jurisdictional chaos and short-term, short-sighted expedients. In these circumstances swift, efficient, even thoughtful government – let alone despotism – was not a serious possibility. After the Revolution it would be different, as Tocqueville saw.

(ii) Social

The destruction of the division of the national representative body into three separate orders of clergy, nobility and third estate was looked upon by the revolutionaries as one of their first, and greatest, achievements. The clergy and the nobility, they believed, represented two unjustly privileged orders within the nation, exempt from many laws and obligations common to all other Frenchmen. There was to be no place for privilege of any sort, let alone privileged orders, under the new constitution. There was some rationale behind the privileges enjoyed by the clergy and the nobility before 1789. It went back to the medieval division of society into those who prayed (the first estate), those who fought (the second), and those who worked (the third) [75]. Noble and clerical tax exemptions were still being justified by reference to this classic principle as late as the mid 1770s, but such arguments were dismissed out of hand by the revolutionaries as specious pleading designed to buttress glaring civil inequalities. Generations of historians showed a rare unanimity in accepting this picture of Ancien Regime society. It is only in the mid twentieth century that its nature and structure have become a subject for serious scholarly discussion and debate.

It began [13] with the publication of a book on French popular uprisings in the seventeenth century by the Soviet Marxist historian Boris Porshnev [85]. Porshnev argued that these uprisings, most of which seemed to have been triggered off by tax-demands , were part of a class struggle of the masses against their feudal exploiters. The state, in his view, was nothing but an instrument of the nobility, the feudal class. 'Feudalo-absolutism' was merely a new way of exploiting peasant production to line the pockets and serve the purposes of the feudal nobility. This remains a standard Marxist view of the social significance of absolute monarchy. For instance, 26 years after Porshnev first wrote, an influential English Marxist was arguing that absolutism was essentially 'a redeployed and recharged apparatus of feudal domination' [105]. As an analysis it has curious similarities with a controversial non-Marxist characterisation of seventeenth-century England as a one-class society, in which there was 'only one body of persons capable of concerted action over the whole area of society' to exercise 'collective power, political and economic' [120]. The proponent of this idea would, however, deny that there were any other classes in a position to struggle against it; and Roland Mousnier has denied that the Marxist analysis describes any of the realities of seventeenth-century French society.

21

Mousnier was outraged to see the state depicted as the instrument of any social group. The nobility, so far from controlling the monarchy, had always been its greatest opponent, and on closer inspection most of Porshnev's popular uprisings would be found to have noble leaders and instigators [82]. To admit that the monarchy was a mere tool of the nobility would be to rob it of much of its glory and diminish the coherence of the authoritarian interpretation of its history, of which Mousnier was now the leading custodian. Mousnier launched a phalanx of pupils into the archives to investigate seventeenth-century popular uprisings in a depth beyond anything Porshnev could have achieved; but meanwhile he saw that the Russian's position rested as much on a theory of society as on empirical evidence about uprisings. He determined to elaborate a counter-theory more in accordance with ascertainable seventeenth-century conditions, and he found a basis for it in the writings of the American sociologist Bernard Barber, and one of his beloved jurists, Charles Loyseau (1564–1627) [14]. Loyseau spent a lifetime minutely anatomising the various orders that contemporary French society was divided into. It was not simply a matter of clergy, nobility and third estate. Within each order or estate there were innumerable hierarchical subdivisions corresponding to precise social and professional functions, and Loyseau listed them in order of rank and prestige. Mousnier thought such a contemporary description far closer to reality than any characterisation of seventeenth-century society based on classes. It was, rather, a society of orders. Such a society

consists of a hierarchy of degrees ... distinguished from one another and arranged not according to the wealth of their members and the latters' capacity to consume, and not according to their role in the production of material goods, but according to the esteem, honour, and dignity attached by society to social functions that can have no relationship with the production of material goods [81].

A society of classes, on the other hand,

appears in a market economy, when supreme social value is placed in the production of material goods, and when supreme social esteem, honour and social dignity go to he who undertakes such production, and when it is the role played in the mode of production of material goods and secondarily the money earned by this role which places individuals at the various levels in the social hierarchy.

This theory colours the study of Ancien Regime society in two ways. In the first place Mousnier contends that different orders were often in conflict, as the prestige accorded by society to their functions changed. In feudal society (which, unlike the Marxists, he thinks had disappeared by the sixteenth century) the warrior enjoyed undisputed prestige, and from this derived the prescriptive social pre-eminence of the nobility of the sword. Subsequently, as the state became more sophisticated, lawyers and administrators acquired an increasingly important role, and came to constitute a rival supreme order in the form of the nobility of the robe. They never won clear superiority, but by the eighteenth century they had certainly achieved parity. This conclusion had earlier been reached, from a different starting point, by the American historian Franklin Ford [77]. But by the eighteenth century too – and this is the second implication of Mousnier's theory – the society of orders was in decline. Increasing prosperity had nurtured within it an expanding commercial bourgeoisie whose claim to consideration rested entirely upon liquid wealth. What they wanted was a society of classes, and in 1789 they overthrew the old society of orders to get it. In this way Mousnier neatly brought his new theory of Ancien Regime society into line with traditional, and Marxist, interpretations of the motivations behind the Revolution of 1789. Unfortunately, by this time such interpretations were themselves in ruins.

There had never been any disputing that the men who overthrew the Ancien Regime were bourgeois, in the sense that they were not nobles. Marxists, and many others since Jaurès, have tended to argue in addition that they were bourgeois in the sense of representing capitalism and non-landed wealth. In social terms, the most important achievement of the Ancien Regime had been to prepare and nurture the capitalistic bourgeoisie for its assumption of power in

23

1789. Between 1954 and 1964, however, Alfred Cobban argued [35] vigorously that the third estate deputies elected in 1789, who formed the majority in the National Assembly that dismantled the Ancien Regime, had had very few capitalists or men of liquid wealth among their numbers. They were in fact mostly lawyers, office-holders and men of property. Meanwhile George V. Taylor was arguing that most of the bourgeoisie in pre-revolutionary France were men of this sort [95], and that capitalism was a minority source of wealth. In the 1780s the French bourgeoisie was overwhelmingly non-commercial, and even those members of it who were not were anxious to leave trade and industry as soon as their wealth permitted them decently to do so. And this was a very traditional pattern, what some historians have called the 'defection' or 'treason' of the bourgeoisie [108]. The whole success of venal offices since the sixteenth century had depended upon the bourgeois desire to invest commercial profits in status. Their entire scale of values was not that of a separate class at all. It was dictated by the anti-commercial value system of the nobility. Even privilege, which supposedly cut clergy and nobility irreconcilably off from the rest of the nation before the Revolution, was something in which the bourgeoisie shared. Betty Behrens has argued [35] that privilege was a principle that ran throughout Ancien Regime society, and benefited almost everybody in it, directly or indirectly. Elsewhere she points out that not even the supposed exemption from taxation of the 'privileged orders' was complete, and that in this respect the most privileged persons in France might well have been certain bourgeois [70].

The fact that bourgeois could aspire to nobility implied something else: that they had a reasonable chance of achieving it. Revolutionary propaganda portrayed the old nobility as a closed caste, impenetrable to outsiders. Improbable demographically, this picture has now been shown to be false empirically as well [72]. Thanks largely to ennoblement through venal office, it was always easy for rich commoners to buy themselves into the second order; nor were poor nobles usually too proud to 'regild their arms' by marrying bourgeois heiresses. Throughout Ancien Regime society, wealth could overcome almost any social barrier. And so what had inhibited the 'career open to the talents' demanded by the revolutionaries of 1789 was not so much birth as money, and their protest was (unwittingly) against the Ancien Regime's social mobility rather than its rigidity.

None of this was new in the later eighteenth century. Recruitment of bourgeois into the nobility, and constant ennoblement of bourgeois wealth were structural features of Ancien Regime society, as eye-catching in the sixteenth century as in the eighteenth. Yet for all that something important had changed by the latter period. Whereas the numbers of the nobility had remained fairly constant, the bourgeoisie had expanded enormously in the unprecedented commercial prosperity of the eighteenth century. Rising prices for land and venal offices [74] suggest that this expansion was not accompanied by any great change in traditional aspirations in the form of a turning away from the time-honoured preference for proprietary over liquid wealth. Yet opportunities for ennoblement did not increase. This meant that more bourgeois than ever were leading lives like noblemen, though without the technical status. Nobles and bourgeois became less and less distinguishable from one another. Increasingly, nobility came to seem merely a special set of privileges that certain men of property happened to have, but these privileges no longer marked off a coherent class or social group [78]. In this sense the importance of the traditional orders of society certainly was on the wane. The noble order, which had once constituted France's unchallenged social elite, had been replaced, or rather absorbed by what it seems perfectly fair to call a class. What is less than adequate is to call it the bourgeois class. Most of its members certainly were bourgeois in Ancien Regime terms, but not in Marxist ones, so historians wishing to avoid further confusions have sought a new name. In the 1960s, in recognition of the cultural homogeneity the group derived from its common educational experience, many adopted the term 'Enlightenment elite' (*l'élite des lumières*) [67]. In the 1970s, others began to be struck by its similarity to the group which emerged to rule France between the time of Napoleon and 1848, basing its members' entitlement to political rights on their landed property as measured by tax-assessments. They were known as the *Notables*, and the

25

name has now been generally adopted to describe the pre-revolutionary upper class who were their obvious ancestors [71]. Those who accept this analysis, and the less than satisfactory nomenclature that goes with it, see the Revolution as the seizure of power by this class in the aftermath of the financial collapse of absolute monarchy. The adoption of the Estates-General, an assembly divided into traditional orders, arbitrarily resurrected distinctions and power-structures which social development since its last meeting in 1614 had rendered obsolete [80]. So the first task was to get rid of them. That done, the deputies could set about creating a regime in which sovereignty lay with a national assembly representing the solid men of property who had already come together as France's effective governing class over the preceding century.

(iii) Economic

The men of 1789 believed in a free market economy. They removed controls on the grain trade and only reimposed them for a time under popular pressure. They abolished trade guilds and prohibited trade unions as unnatural impediments to free market relations. They also abolished a whole range of burdens on agriculture in the form of rights, dues and fees payable to lords under the general name of the 'feudal regime' or 'feudalism'. In the eyes of Marx and his disciples, all this made the Revolution a major economic turning point, when the forces of capitalism burst asunder the fetters of the feudal organisation of agriculture and manufacturing industry. The Revolution therefore brought to an end not only a distinctive political structure, and a particular form of society, but also a stage in economic development. Economically, it was the end of the middle ages; and the Ancien Regime, during which the forces of capitalism steadily built themselves up to the point of triumph, was the beginning of the end.

This interpretation has not survived the onslaught of mid-twentieth-century criticism. It has been pointed out that from the 1760s onwards governments had themselves been groping towards free trade in grain and the abolition of trade guilds, and had never countenanced any form of worker organisations. And one of the central points of Cobban's attack on then-received opinion was that the National Assembly had had to be forced into abolishing feudal dues in August 1789 by pressure from an overburdened peasantry. In any case, what by 1789 men called feudal bore little relation to what had gone by that name in the middle ages. By the time of the Revolution feudalism as a form of economic organisation had long vanished. Its surviving relics were nothing more than a surcharge on landed property, and not evidence of a still-vital economic relationship. Nobody now lived off feudal dues as lords had done in medieval times. Nor did the men of 1789 even think they were changing the basic structure of the economy. Indeed, they were hoping to strengthen it. Their determination to throw off the economic paternalism of the Ancien Regime state was derived from the arguments of the Physiocrats. Quesnay, Mirabeau, Le Mercier de la Rivière, Turgot and Dupont de Nemours argued that agriculture was the sole expandable source of wealth, and therefore to be impeded as little as possible. But it was industrialisation, which the Physiocrats thought a dead-end, that was destined to revolutionise economic life.

The Marxist picture of the Ancien Regime as the last stage of the feudal economy has, therefore, largely been abandoned. But the initial attractions of Marxism gave enormous stimulus to detailed research on economic history, and this has transformed our understanding of how the economy of the Ancien Regime worked. The first important results came in the history of prices. The economist François Simiand in 1932 staked out the broad outlines of price history from the sixteenth to the nineteenth century [93]. An 'A phase' of rising prices over the sixteenth century gave way in the course of the early seventeenth to a 'B phase' in which they stagnated or fell. Around 1730 a new A phase began which went on until the early 1820s. But these broad trends were punctuated by 'intercycles' when momentum flagged, and this phenomenon was illustrated by the researches of Ernest Labrousse for the eighteenth century [87, 88]. Labrousse confirmed in massive detail for France that an overall rise in prices did begin in the 1730s, and that the mid eighteenth century was a time of surging prosperity. But around 1770 a period of difficulties set

27

in, and they reached their acutest form in 1788–9. Tocqueville and Jaurès had therefore been wrong to depict the Revolution as breaking out amid unprecedented prosperity. France was undoubtedly richer than she had ever been, following phenomenal mid-century expansion; but the 1780s were a time of crisis and widespread hardship. At the root of the crisis lay inadequate harvests. Their effect was to push up the price of staple foodstuffs, which created hardship for all wage-earners; but more spent on food meant less spent on manufactures, and thus a fall in demand. Unemployment accordingly rose, and wages became vulnerable. Debtors defaulted, and credit was shaken throughout the economy. Nor, Labrousse argued, was what happened in the 1780s a unique and unparalleled crisis, except perhaps in its intensity. In any overwhelmingly agricultural economy with poor communications, activity must be highly regionalised owing to prohibitive transport costs. His own researches on prices revealed wide regional disparities, and since he wrote others have laid increasing emphasis on the 'two Frances' of the Ancien Regime. The relatively prosperous littoral and its hinterland were linked in by rivers and the sea to international trading networks, and cushioned against local famines; but the interior was a collection of isolated, poor and regionally oriented economies only tenuously connected with one another and the outside world. In the north and west agriculture was relatively advanced and market-oriented from an early stage. In the centre and south it remained backward and crisis-prone down to 1789 and far beyond [91].

In the economic Ancien Regime, the manufacturing sector was always secondary to the agricultural, and in the last analysis dependent on its prosperity. After all, most consumers of manufactures, whether governments, ruling orders or ordinary people, largely lived off the profits of agriculture. Most taxes and rents came out of the pockets of peasants working the soil. But until late in the eighteenth century the state left agriculture largely to its own devices, because ministers like Colbert were convinced that manufactures were the true way to enrich the state. By producing all it needed a state could avoid dependence on foreign imports; by producing more than it needed it could bring in the wealth of others by exporting. And by protecting, regulating and supervising crucial economic sectors a government could make them flourish. The nineteenth century was to call such policies mercantilism. Even when the Physiocrats had convinced Louis XV's and Louis XVI's ministers of the superior claims of agriculture, they never gave up the habits of regulation inherited from the seventeenth century. State regulation, as Tocqueville pointed out, was a basic feature of the Ancien Regime economy.

And yet the most important type of manufacture was among the most difficult to supervise and regulate. The only large-scale industry with a guaranteed mass market was textiles. In the late middle ages most textiles for more than local consumption had been produced in urban workshops subject to guild regulation. In some areas, such as the luxury silk trade of Lyons, this system persisted throughout the Ancien Regime. But by the mid seventeenth century most textiles were being produced in the countryside, and only marketed from the towns, under the domestic, 'putting out' or *verlag* system of manufacture. Low on capital costs, this system largely escaped guild restriction and found a ready labour force in peasants barely subsisting from agriculture. Ancien Regime industry was, therefore, 'pre-industrial' in the sense that most goods were produced on a small scale, in small workshops, using little power beyond that of human muscles. Concentrated production grew increasingly common in the eighteenth century, but even by the end it still only accounted for a tiny proportion of manufacturing output. And the form it took was that of the 'proto-factory', concentrating existing types of productive capacity in one place. Powering new capacity on a large scale with inanimate sources of energy – factory production proper – still lay largely in the future.

Labour, after all, was cheap; increasingly so in a century of rising population. The scale of this rise is now fairly well known thanks to a massive expansion of work in historical demography over the last generation. It now seems that the population of France had risen from 21½ million around 1700 to over 28 million in 1789, 2 million more than the figure generally given until a few years ago [86]. This rise began in the context of a pattern which has come to be called the

29

demographic or biological Ancien Regime [109,117]. This pattern was one of late marriage (at 25 on average for men and rather less for women) and rapid remarriage among the widowed. Far fewer people remained single than in subsequent ages, and illegitimacy was rare too. The rate of legitimate births remained remarkably constant at one about every two years, with very little evidence of artificial limitation except in restricted, and usually superior, social groups. But although fertility could be expected to last until a wife's early 40s, the average size of families was not strikingly high: usually between 4 and 5 children. This was because of high rates of mortality. The demographic Ancien Regime was characterised by very high infant mortality: only half the children born ever grew to adulthood. Adult mortality was higher than in modern times, too, but its key feature was violent fluctuation. What held the population back was the effect of periodic severe demographic crises, when deaths rose to double or treble the normal number, while marriages and births fell away. When the crisis was over, the latter would resume at compensatory rates, but a severe crisis could nevertheless mark the demographic character of a whole generation. At the root of most demographic crises, like economic ones more generally, lay deficient harvests. One poor year might be ridden out, but a succession, in which reserves and seed stocks were run down, could culminate in starvation or at least chronic undernourishment which left all except the strongest particularly vulnerable to disease. The worst crises came when famine and epidemics, exacerbated by the disruptions of war, struck together, but demography, like most other things in the economic Ancien Regime, was extremely localised. Nation-wide crises almost never occurred. Few were more than regional in scale, and most were little more than local. But they happened so frequently, in so many areas, that the overall population of the country seemed unable to rise beyond a ceiling of about 20 million, and was repeatedly forced back whenever it approached this level. Only in the eighteenth century did the pattern begin to change.

There were significant differences, finally, between the demographic characteristics of town and country. Urban death rates were higher, and indeed almost always exceeded birth rates. For towns to keep up their size, therefore, much less to grow, their population had to be replenished by immigration, and studies of urban parish registers invariably show that most of those who died in a town had not been born there. Historians, even leading demographic ones [89], have been slow to abandon the semi-romantic picture of sedentary rural life, with the vast majority of the population passing their whole existence within narrow local horizons and time-less local routines. It is becoming increasingly clear, however, that the constant tendency of rural areas to become overpopulated for the resources available was offset not only by demographic crises, but by steady and regular emigration, either temporary or permanent. At any moment, important proportions of the country population must have been on the road in search of work. In an economy constricted by high transport costs, human beings found it easier to move themselves than most other things.

(iv) Cultural

The men of 1789 were rationalisers. They wished to create a France where everything was reasonable, logical and clear in organisation, and just, economical and useful in purpose. They saw the Ancien Regime as a rubbish heap of chaos, illogicality, routine, waste and injustice, and the outlook which sustained it as a blend of selfishness, superstition and fanaticism. This point of view was what Taine condemned as the 'classic spirit' that had subverted the Ancien Regime, making no allowance for the complexities of social evolution, and even basic human psychology. But it, too, was a product of the Ancien Regime, however unpalatable Taine might find the thought. The Ancien Regime mentality, historians are coming to realise, was quite as complex in character as its other facets.

The Ancien Regime was a Roman Catholic regime. The established, state religion was Catholicism, the highest title of the 'Most Christian king' to his throne was that God had put him there, and to God alone was he accountable. His reign began with a coronation at which he swore to protect the church and persecute heretics, and was anointed with the sacred oil of Clovis originally brought down from Heaven by a holy dove. The blood of St Louis (Louis IX) ran in his veins. His subjects all passed their lives in the shadow of the church, too, both physically and metaphorically. It dictated the calendar; baptised, married and buried everybody; monopolised education; organised medical services and poor relief; and owned most of the largest buildings and a tenth of the land of France. All this was shattered between 1790 and 1801, and never entirely put together again. To embattled Catholics looking back from later ages, the Ancien Regime appeared a time of simple faith and piety, of spiritual consensus and harmony. But this view always depended on deliberately discounting certain of its obvious features.

One was the existence of important religious minorities, above all the Huguenots. Protestantism was in fact as old as the Ancien Regime itself, and was illegal only for its last century. Even then it retained a dwindling number of adherents, largely concentrated in the south and the Rhenish provinces. But in Catholic eyes, then and since, Protestants were an alien body, un-French, rebellious by nature, responsible for civil war in the sixteenth century, insurrection in the seventeenth, and (according to some) revolution in the eighteenth [17]. Few modern historians would go so far, but Ancien Regime Protestants still tend to be regarded as an 'unassimilable minority' [38], and their achievement of toleration in the 1780s as a sign of weakening faith and the decline of religious values [32]. Yet Protestants played an important part in developing French overseas commerce, organised and controlled much of the Languedoc cloth industry, and in the eighteenth century Huguenot bankers and their overseas contacts were crucial in keeping the state financially afloat [90]. Without the Protestants, whether as a threat or a stimulus, the whole development of the Ancien Regime would have been different. They were an integral part of it.

And so was fierce conflict within the Catholic Church. Pre-revolutionary times were not the picture of unquestioning uniformity dreamed of by credulous nineteenth- and twentieth-century romantics. The frontiers between the respective

32

spheres of church and state were a central preoccupation of Ancien Regime politics almost down to the eve of the Revolution. This was because quarrelling churchmen constantly appealed to the authority either of the king or his courts to resolve their disputes. Most of these centred around the authority of the Pope in France, and between 1540 and 1764 his main supporters were the Jesuits. With royal support they mostly held their own against enemies in the parlements, the universities, and among certain other religious orders. But their determination to crush all enemies, actual or potential, had the effect of creating a loose coalition against them, which came to be called Jansenism. Confined in the seventeenth century to a restricted circle of the educated, by the 1720s Jansenism was attracting mass support. Between the mid 1740s and the mid 1760s issues raised by the Jansenist controversy dominated public affairs, and died away only after the Jesuits were expelled from the kingdom in 1764. But by then stands had been taken, and positions formulated, that there was no going back on; and the early religious history of the Revolution was full of echoes of the conflicts and controversies of mid-century.

Both sides in the great religious conflict opened up by the Revolution could agree about one thing at least: much of the blame for what had gone wrong could be put on the Ancien Regime educational system. Catholics condemned it for allowing irreligion to spread; revolutionaries accused it of perpetuating superstition and fanaticism. Modern historians, however, now see the Ancien Regime as a time when educational provision in French society expanded dramatically under the stimulus of the printed word, Catholic determination to combat heresy, and public demand [98]. Basic literacy, enjoyed by only about a fifth of the population under Louis XIV, took in about a third by Louis XVI's time. By the end of the seventeenth century the upper echelons of society were all fully literate, and the number of colleges catering to their demand had grown steadily since the mid sixteenth century. At every level education was controlled by the church, and the increase in educational standards over the whole period of the Ancien Regime was perhaps the greatest achievement of the Catholic Counter-Reformation.

Thus France was saved from Protestantism, which made few converts after the early seventeenth century. It was not, however, saved, as we have already seen, from disagreements about what good Catholic practice was. Knowledge might be the antidote to heresy, but it also made men more critical about orthodoxy. Few disputed, even in the eighteenth century, that the faith should be strengthened. The problem was how to strengthen it without changing it, and on this there was little agreement. There was certainly a sustained attempt to purify popular religion by stamping out pagan survivals which had gone largely unquestioned before the Reformation; but this was a battle far from won in 1789, as might be expected in a country where the vast majority were still illiterate peasants, and where indeed only a third of the population spoke recognisable French at all. The rest spoke thick dialects or, as in Brittany or the Basque country, entirely distinct languages. In any case every locality had its own saints, relics, holy wells and traditions, practices and ceremonies connected with them. To eliminate this enormous diversity would have demanded an effort and resources quite beyond the Ancien Regime church, even if it could have formulated an agreed approach. It was easier to impose uniformity on the elites, through the Latinised education of the colleges, but even here the 'Baroque Piety' of the Counter-Reformation had begun to crumble by the mid eighteenth century. In Provence from that time onwards, when men made their wills they tended to begin them with fewer pious invocations, to endow fewer masses for their souls, and to make fewer charitable bequests. During life they lit fewer holy candles, and tended to desert the penitential and other religious brotherhoods that had flourished since the sixteenth century. Adopting a description from the Revolution, the historian of these tendencies calls them signs of dechristianisation, and argues that they make revolutionary attacks on the established church more comprehensible. The way had been prepared for half a century [103]. Others argue that such signs are merely evidence of a changed attitude to religious practice rather than a decline in depth of belief. Religion that was less outward was perhaps more profoundly inward [115]. Less emphasis on devout practices did not necessarily imply less concern for practical, everyday Christian living. Even a well-attested eighteenth-century decline in religious vocations and entries into the priesthood has been characterised as a 'secularisation of religious attitudes', a turning away from the priestly ideal rather than from the truths of Christianity itself [100]. And the great revolutionary quarrel with the church, most historians would agree, was quite unpremeditated. It began as an attempt to purge the church of a whole range of attributes and practices which the men of 1789 thought weakened its moral authority within the nation. It was the refusal of a large segment of the priesthood, encouraged by the Pope himself, to accept changes on this scale which sparked off the conflict.

Many Catholics in retrospect, however, accepted Edmund Burke's argument that the attack on the church was planned in advance by the writers of the Enlightenment; and until quite recently it was generally accepted that the Enlightenment was deeply hostile to, and therefore in some sense not part of, the Ancien Regime. It was, after all, a movement of criticism. Writers like Voltaire and works like Diderot's *Encyclopédie* criticised the church above all, but no established institution or outlook escaped discussion in the unprecedented torrent of print that marked the eighteenth century. Yet to criticise is not to condemn out of hand, and it seems increasingly clear that what both the producers and the consumers of the Enlightenment wanted was improvement, not destruction. To a man, the critics of the established church and its doctrines were products of priest-run schools, the finest flower of the Counter-Reformation. The tacit protection of government ensured that their works were printed and distributed without serious impediment, despite occasional bursts of repression. Their reputations were made as much by what was said about them in the *salons* of Parisian high society as by what they wrote; and by the 1760s the *philosophes* had taken over all the main organs and institutions of national intellectual life. They had become a literary establishment [96]. The main consumers of their works, too, were members of the social elites – nobles, magistrates, office-holders, lawyers. They it was, in the provinces, who bought the books [97], read the journals, joined the libraries and established the academies, literary societies and masonic lodges through which the ideals and values of the Enlightenment were disseminated [102]. They did not feel threatened by the thought of their time. They quite obviously did not expect it to lead to the sort of upheavals that began in 1789 and were to destroy their status, privileges, offices and indeed most of the cultural institutions they patronised. It was only when those upheavals got under way, and people strove to explain what had brought such momentous changes about, that the Enlightenment began to be singled out as a force for subversion. Such a conclusion seemed all the more obvious when most of the revolutionaries openly claimed to be instruments in the triumph of 'philosophy'. The bodies of Voltaire and (later) Rousseau were disinterred and reburied in the new Pantheon, and they and other critical writers of the Ancien Regime were constantly invoked as prophets and progenitors of what was now being done [99]. In this, again, revolutionaries and their bitterest enemies seemed agreed; and that confronts historians with a problem. If, to all but a few paranoid churchmen, the Enlightenment did not look like a revolutionary ideology before 1789, how could it be so readily recognised as one immediately afterwards? The most convincing answer so far to emerge is that the Revolution made it one [69]. Nobody foresaw the scale of the Ancien Regime's collapse, nor the simultaneous range of opportunities for reform that it would offer. Even at the beginning of 1789 reforming opinion was far less radical than it was to be by midsummer. What produced the revolutionary ideology was the turning of minds steeped in the Enlightenment to the practical problems of simultaneously governing and regenerating a country where public order had almost broken down. Representative institutions brought to power just the sort of people who had been the Enlightenment's audience – a largely uncommercial, landed and professional *élite des lumières*. The mental equipment with which they confronted the problems of government had been formed in the intellectual world the Enlightenment dominated, and it provided the materials from which they put together their revolutionary ideology. It did not, however, provide that ideology ready-made. The Enlightenment was an Ancien Regime phenomenon. The Revolution transformed it by wrenching it, like so much else, into a new and different shape.

36

(v) European

When the men of 1789 first formulated the idea of the Ancien Regime, they were thinking of something French. Very soon, however, as foreign onlookers started to condemn what they were doing, they came to regard the Ancien Regime as an order of things that far transcended the frontiers of France, and remained alive and dangerous beyond them. They saw the war of 1792 as a struggle against the Ancien Regime wherever it existed, and in so far as the other states of Europe made common cause against the aggressive republic, they were implicitly acknowledging that they shared a range of values and institutions akin to those the French had swept away.

Most historians are prepared to accept that to one degree or another this was true. In the fourteenth century, argued Tocqueville, the institutions and social structure of western Europe had been fundamentally the same everywhere. By the eighteenth century, to be sure, this 'ancient constitution of Europe' was 'half in ruins', losing its vitality; but the ruins were everywhere still. And what had brought about their ruin was the same thing too – absolutism, and the growth of the centralised state. Since Tocqueville's time this perspective has provided the title for innumerable textbook surveys of the seventeenth and eighteenth centuries [106,121], and it is certainly true that many European monarchs during that time wielded an authority as absolute as, or more absolute than, the King of France. Between the 1660s and the French Revolution rulers great and small modelled themselves, and the courts they operated from, on Louis XIV and Versailles [125]. But these arguments have their difficulties. As in France, the power of many theoretically absolute monarchs was limited in practice by institutions whose autonomy they were unable for one reason or another to destroy [116]. And in many small states, and a number of large and important ones (such as Sweden, Poland, the Dutch Republic and Great Britain) government was parliamentary. British historians, always reluctant to see their country as part of Europe at all, tend to think such diversity negates any idea of a continent-wide political Ancien Regime [36:20–4]. The American R. R. Palmer argues, however, that the precise way government was organised mattered far less than the sort of people who made it work [124]. It was aristocrats, whether as members of 'constituted bodies' like estates, diets, parliaments or *parlements*, or as the only contenders for office at the courts of absolute monarchs, who governed Europe from the Atlantic to the Urals. Another approach to the problem of the simultaneous existence of different forms of government suggests that all states were involved in the same process of overall development, but were at different stages in it. According to the Marxist Perry Anderson [105], absolutism was the political manifestation of the last stage in the feudal mode of production; in which nobles sought to shore up their crumbling domination of the peasant masses by surrendering some of their power and authority to a strengthened central state, which in turn guaranteed their social position. The bourgeoisie had no real place in this compact, and accordingly once they were strong enough, they overthrew absolutism and feudalism together. That process began in England in the 1640s, continued in France in the 1790s, and spread to the rest of Europe over the subsequent century. All countries, then, had Ancien Regimes, but they were not necessarily contemporaneous. The English version had gone before the others reached their peak.

Tocqueville, too, argued something like this; and one does not need to be a Marxist to agree that the political institutions of the Ancien Regime were in a number of ways embedded in a social and economic structure that was Europe-wide. Down to very recent times the population of all European countries was overwhelmingly rural. Society in all of them was dominated by small groups of landlords enjoying hereditary distinctions. Everywhere the economy was pre-industrial. Agriculture predominated. Economic activity was restricted and regulated by countless controls, customs and restrictive practices. Industry was organised in small-scale productive units, scattered rather than concentrated. The population seemed fated not to rise above what now seems a very modest level without running into the savage Malthusian checks imposed by dearth and disease. This social and economic world has been memorably described at length in the last great work of Fernand Braudel [109]. Closer inspection, of course, reveals innumerable variations in the pattern, and Braudel revels in the task of integrating them. But some present more formidable problems than others. Above all there is the difference between eastern and western Europe. In the west, although many relics of feudalism remained, serfdom had largely disappeared by the sixteenth century. East of the Elbe, on the contrary, it was only first fully imposed around the same time, and its incidence grew heavier down to the eighteenth century. The east was only lightly urbanised, the west heavily. The bourgeoisie in the east was tiny and powerless. In the west, it was the fastest expanding social category in terms of numbers, wealth and education. Western Europe, along the Atlantic seaboard, enriched itself with the products of the Americas and the Indian Ocean, but little of its opulence trickled into the inaccessible world east of the Elbe. And in many ways the gap widened over early modern times [114]. In the face of such yawning discrepancies, to speak of a Europe-wide Ancien Regime in social or economic terms seems meaningless.

It has been argued, however, that these differences were in fact complementary aspects of a greater whole. According to Immanuel Wallerstein [129], enthusiastically followed in this by Braudel, Europe emerged in the sixteenth century as a 'world-economy' or 'world-system' driven by the expansive force of capitalism. The essence of a world-economy is economic differentiation. There are 'core areas' and there are peripheries, and that was the relationship between western and eastern Europe. Capitalism was born, and flourished, in the core areas of the west – in the Dutch Republic, in England, and in France. Everywhere else was peripheral, relegated to primary or low-grade production and doomed to relative poverty. In this perspective eastern Europe, like the Americas, was after all part of a single European economic and social system, but a subordinate part; and that explains its distinct characteristics.

The analyses of Braudel and Wallerstein clearly owe a good deal to Marxism, and nowhere more so than in their emphasis on the growth of capitalism. In their view, this was quite the most signifcant aspect of the economic Ancien Regime. For much of its span, certainly, capitalism was largely confined to

39

trade and commerce, and still little involved in truly productive activities. But as Europe's trade grew to encompass the whole world, capitalism became the motor of accelerating activity on all fronts, ultimately powering the breakthrough into industrialisation that spelled the end of the economic Ancien Regime which had nurtured it. Nor were the consequences of capitalism exclusively economic. By enriching the bourgeoisie in the west and expanding their numbers it altered the balance and shape of society [119], and this in its turn had important cultural implications. A bourgeoisie growing richer and more numerous demanded, and could afford to buy, better education. Ruling aristocracies felt obliged to keep up, and so early modern times were marked throughout western Europe by a widening provision of schools and universities. Their products in turn formed the audience to which the universal, cosmopolitan doctrines of the Enlightenment would appeal. Until well into the eighteenth century the language of advanced education everywhere was Latin, and even when it began to decline its place was taken to some extent by French. In Catholic Europe, international teaching orders such as the Jesuits gave a pattern to the education of the social elites which transcended frontiers. The tastes and needs of this expanding educated elite were met by an increasing output of the printed word. Indeed, in cultural terms, the Ancien Regime might be defined as the period between the invention of printing and the achievement of universal literacy.

The highly educated were not the only groups to be affected. Print had a profound impact on popular culture, providing incentives to become literate and at the same time freezing what had been fluid oral traditions into standardised forms [112]. But there was a buoyant market, in the west at least, for chapbooks and other printed ephemera as popular literacy inched forward. Popular culture, assessed from such sources, often exhibits remarkable similarities from one end of the continent to the other in terms of festivals, rituals, beliefs, and even the stories told in songs, plays and chapbooks. On the other hand, the populace, unlike the social elites who ruled over them, were completely cut off from one another by differing languages and dialects over often quite short distances. Above all there was wide religious diversity, especially in countries won over in the sixteenth century to Protestantism. Another way of defining the cultural Ancien Regime would be as the period between the Reformation and the advent of sustained attacks on organised religion, when the confessional unity of the middle ages had gone, and rival religious establishments sought to strengthen their control over their adherents. In this context, all churches were intolerant towards rivals, anxious to indoctrinate the faithful with correct opinions, and to impose moral restraint on more extreme manifestations of popular culture – a movement that has been described as the 'triumph of Lent' [112].

There was, finally, one way in which all Europe was bound up in a single system that is so obvious it risks being overlooked. This is the interrelationship between states. The idea of a diplomatic Ancien Regime was propounded by the Frenchman Albert Sorel in 1885 in the first volume of his monumental *L'Europe et la Révolution Française*[127]. Sorel, it is true, confined his Ancien Regime to the eighteenth century, when states no longer fought for religion, justice or other high principles, but merely for power, transient advantage and *raison d'état*. His overall aim was, like Tocqueville's, to show that the Revolution fundamentally changed nothing, and that beneath the spectacular upheavals on the surface deeper trends apparent beforehand soon resurfaced. The deepest trend, however, he neglected – the progressive refinement of military technology. Between 1560 and 1660, it has been argued, Europe witnessed a 'military revolution' which 'stands like great divide separating medieval society from the modern world' [126]. As firearms became more dependable and more manoeuvrable, linear tactics were adopted both on the battlefield and at sea. Success now came to depend on technique and technology rather than weight of numbers, and this put a premium on discipline and professionalism.

The logic of such developments led to standing armed forces, using standardised equipment. Once a major state like France adopted these principles in the mid seventeenth century, rivals or emulators could not afford to be left behind, and so by the beginning of the eighteenth century standing armies and navies were almost universal. The ramifications were equally inexorable. Up-to-date armed forces were very expensive and constantly consumed huge quantities of a wide range of resources. They had to be recruited, paid, clothed, fed, housed and equipped even in peacetime. Governments, accordingly, had to take much closer control of their territories and populations to ensure that the necessary resources were always to hand. They now needed manpower policies, mining and metallurgical policies, woodland policies (for shipbuilding), strategic transport policies, food-growing policies, and foreign policies geared to securing or protecting supplies that they lacked. The coercive power of standing armies in itself, of course, brought an important advance in the state's control over society. Above all, these things needed to be paid for, and states found themselves attempting to tap ever-growing proportions of their subjects' wealth through taxation, or borrowing, or most commonly both. Sometimes, as in England, it was achieved by consent. More often rulers preferred to override or bypass representative institutions – often with the help of the very armed forces the taxation was to pay for. These imperatives were surely much more important than the greed of feudal landlords in the emergence of absolute monarchy. But the process was imposing enormous strains on all militarily active states by the later eighteenth century. In Russia the steady advance of the central power provoked the colossal Pugachev rebellion of the mid 1770s. The British attempt to tax the American colonies for defence led straight to the War of Independence. Emperor Joseph II's attempts to rationalise his chaotic dominions to make them more competitive internationally had brought Belgium to outright rebellion and Hungary to the brink of it by the time he died in 1790. And France, the great power that had led Europe into military professionalisation, was by then caught up in headlong revolution, a revolution that began with the collapse of an Ancien Regime no longer able to pay for its international ambitions without transforming French society and institutions beyond recognition [116].

3 The Limits of the Ancien Regime

The Ancien Regime was a European phenomenon; a stage in the political, economic, social and cultural evolution of Europe. But what was Europe? Geographers themselves only pushed it to the Urals in the course of the eighteenth century; and a case could be made for excluding Russia, with its distinctive religion and semi-Asiatic political and social structure, from any Europe-wide definition of the Ancien Regime – at least until the eighteenth century, when that regime was already beginning to crumble further west [109,118]. And nobody would accept inclusion of the Turkish-ruled Balkans. It has sometimes been argued that European colonies in America before independence were part of the mother continent's Ancien Regime [124,129], and there are of course certain senses in which they were linked. These colonies were established and controlled by Ancien Regime states; the wealth they helped to produce profoundly influenced the economic and social development of their parent countries; many of their institutions were modelled on European patterns; and their achievement of independence was inextricably bound up with the disintegration of the Ancien Regime in Europe. Yet colonial conditions – geographical, climatic and racial – meant that from the start European models had to be amended almost beyond recognition, and the resulting differences did not diminish with the passage of time. That was why, when it came, independence seemed so logical. Early modern colonial life is, therefore, probably best thought of as a product rather than an integral part of the Ancien Regime. It lay outside its geographical limits.

Even to be a product of the Ancien Regime, however, colonisation must have originated within its chronological limits. That means the Ancien Regime itself must have begun before 1492, at the latest.

(i) Beginnings

Men of the eighteenth century, among whom Frenchmen of 1789 were no exception, thought of the modern world, the world they had been born into, as beginning around 1500. Within half a century on either side of that date the Renaissance revived a spirit of enquiry to which the Enlightenment traced its own ancestry; printing was invented; America was discovered and a sea-route to the east opened up; the Turks took control of south-eastern Europe; and the Reformation shattered the unity of the church. These changes seemed to mark modern times decisively off from the middle ages. Men were conscious of still living with their consequences. Their perspective lives on in the conventional labelling of the years between about 1500 and 1800 as the 'early modern' period. (In France it is called the modern period. History since 1789 is known as contemporary.)

But some of the key features of European life in this period went back much further than the century straddling 1500. The Catholic Church was rooted in antiquity, and the organisational, geographical and economic principles on which it was still based in 1789 were all well established before the year 1000. So was the domination of society by a landed nobility: several eighteenth-century nobilities traced their authority back to conquest in early medieval times, not always without some justification [123]. And feudalism as a form of economic organisation was fully developed, and some would say already in decline, long before the fifteenth century. Considerations of this sort have led certain historians to abandon, or at least treat as secondary, the division of the second millenium AD into medieval and early modern times. For Marxists, the Ancien Regime is above all the time of the feudal mode of production. In that sense it began, or fully emerged, in the aftermath of the Carolingian empire in the ninth century [104]. Few non-Marxists would go back that far. But Dietrich Gerhard [118], who sees the basic institutions of Europe (excluding Russia and the Balkans) lasting unchanged for almost eight centuries, believes that they 'crystallised' between the eleventh and thirteenth centuries. Then it was that invasions came to an end, population began to increase, and new technology was introduced in transport, building and milling. Monarchical states began to emerge and impose order on large stretches of the continent, and with increased security urbanisation resumed after centuries of retreat. It was during this time, too, that organisation into hereditary, functional estates or orders came to characterise society. Meanwhile, the omnipresence of a powerful, self-confident church lent Europe an overarching sense of unity.

This interpretation in its turn is strongly influenced by the work of French non-Marxist (or ex-Marxist) economic historians, the so-called *Annales* School. For them the movement of population is the most fundamental motor of history, and they feel able to locate the start of the demographic old regime, at least, with a good deal of precision. It begins with the Black Death of the mid fourteenth century; the first, and greatest epidemic of the sort that was only to disappear in the course of the eighteenth century. Sweeping in from the east, it was a harbinger of the 'microbic unification' of the world which would keep population levels limited for three hundred years [89, 109]. Tocqueville, approaching history from a very different perspective, also saw the fourteenth century as the starting point from which the long decay of liberty that was the essence of the Ancien Regime could be traced.

Few historians of the French original that gave all other Anciens Regimes their name go even that far back. Absolute monarchy, and the weakness of representative institutions that was its corollary, cannot be traced in France much beyond the last decades of the fifteenth century [27, 58] – although some would argue that it was not until the mid seventeenth century that the triumph of the one and the defeat of the other became irrevocable [59, 64]. Matters hung in the balance throughout the troubled century from the death of Henry II (1559) to the majority of Louis XIV (1661). The Gallican Church attacked by the Revolution, however ancient its economic and organisational pattern, had little else in common with its medieval ancestor. Its relationship with the king and the Pope had been transformed in 1516 by the Concordat of Bologna, and its outlook on the world profoundly marked, again in the sixteenth century, by the experience of the Reformation and Counter-Reformation. And the most fundamental of all the socio-political institutions destroyed in 1789, venality of office, first became widespread in the sixteenth century, too. It is true that venality in public life began to take root in the fifteenth century, and that full heredity of office was not institutionalised until 1604. But when Francis 1 created the *Parties Casuelles* department in 1522 to handle the revenue from venality, its importance both to the government and to society was clear, and it was to remain central down to 1789 itself [74].

Most historians of France would agree, therefore, that the term Ancien Regime is appropriate to describe the sixteenth and seventeenth, as well as the eighteenth centuries. The one recent exception is Betty Behrens. What the men of 1789 thought they were abolishing, in her view, was a system replete with abuses. 'Implicit in the term', she goes on, with questionable logic, 'is thus the idea of decay' [36: *10*]. The Ancien Regime was accordingly only that time during which men were conscious that things could not last. This feeling she traces back only to 1748, when England began to draw ahead in international competition and the Enlightenment's critique of existing ways began to make some impact. But whether the permanence of British power or the overthrow of the existing order seemed in the least probable to contemporaries remains arguable; Pierre Goubert, the most distinguished recent French authority on the Ancien Regime, dismisses the suggestion that it only began in 1748 as a 'misinterpretation unacceptable even from a first-year student' [40]. For Goubert, 1748, so far from being the start of the Ancien Regime, was much more like the end, or at least the beginning of the end.

(ii) Endings

The French Revolution brought to an end, forever, a unique combination of political, social, economic and cultural features that had given France its distinctive character since the sixteenth century. Few contemporaries foresaw the cataclysm before it happened, and none of those predicted or planned for its sweeping scale or tumultuous character. But with hind-sight historians can see that the Ancien Regime was coming under unprecedented strains from around the mid eighteenth century [40:*vol.2*]. International competition was stretching the state's resources and overloading its financial system. An expanding, educated reading public looked on with decreasing confidence, questioning and discussing all received opinion on every imaginable subject. The population rose to unprecedented levels, and while the gap between rich and poor widened, old divisions of status between rich and rich in the upper reaches of society were losing importance. The Revolution resulted from some of these trends, and merely coincided with others [43]. But they, and still others like them, brought the Ancien Regime far more effectively to an end than any set of revolutionary decrees.

Some of these deeper tendencies, on the other hand, took until long after the revolution to work themselves out. This helps to explain the fact that many of the features of the Ancien Regime that the men of 1789 tried to abolish resurfaced when the upheavals of the 1790s were over. The most obvious was monarchy itself. The Revolution took three years to become republican, and France was only to be a republic for 16 out of the 81 years between 1789 and 1870. Even after the establishment of the Third Republic, monarchical parties remained strong for many years. Not even *absolute* monarchy disappeared for good in 1789. The authority of the Emperor Napoleon was far wider in fact than anything the Bourbon kings had enjoyed; and his nephew Napoleon III was little constrained by constitutional limitations. Even the parliamentary monarchy of the Restoration had powers that would have shocked the constitution-makers of 1789. This was what Tocqueville meant when he argued that the historic function of the Revolution was to remove the remaining obstacles in the way of despotism. The men of 1789 had sought to confine the power of the state within clear and inflexible limits. They swept away old ones, convinced of their inadequacy. Inadequate or not, they proved impossible to replace. Traces of certain other institutions supposedly abolished in 1789 did indeed reappear later. The legal profession was allowed to revive a form of venality for certain offices. Indirect taxation and state monopolies, universally execrated and condemned by the early revolutionaries, began to creep back as early as the Directory. By the Concordat of 1801 Napoleon reinstituted a Catholic state church which was only to be disestablished in 1905. In all these spheres, and many others too, the Revolution did not prove to be the definitive break with the old political and institutional order that its participants intended. Yet no institution that survived, or revived later, did so intact or untransformed. They were mere shadows of their former selves, and much of the context within which they had formerly operated had gone. It therefore still seems fair to conclude that the political Ancien Regime of France really did end with the Revolution.

That the Revolution was a comparable social break seems far less obvious. It certainly abandoned the legal framework of orders into which French society was officially organised. Nobility was abolished; privilege was abolished. Yet Napoleon created a new nobility, and under the Restoration what was left of the old one enjoyed an Indian Summer. Titles are still regularly flaunted in present-day France. But with the abolition of venality nobility became what it never had been before, a closed caste, impenetrable except by usurpation. As with nineteenth-century political survivals, superficial continuities concealed deeper transformations. The deepest of all, however, pre-dated the Revolution by at least half a century – the emergence of that unified social elite of landed proprietors which the post-revolutionary world would call the *Notables*. The Revolution, by abolishing the counter-attraction of venal offices, and marketing unprecedented amounts of confiscated church and *émigré* lands at a time of economic disruption, merely confirmed and accelerated this landed group's consolidation [71]. Trade and industry commanded as little social prestige in the early nineteenth century as they had since the remotest times. And in that sense it might be more appropriate to regard the rule of the *Notables* as the last phase of the old order rather than the first of a new. The old nobility might have been absorbed into a wider entity, but the outlook and values of this greater group still largely derived from noble ones. Only when landowners ceased to enjoy automatic precedence could the social Ancien Regime be said to be disappearing.

This was only likely to happen when the whole economy became transformed. It is now generally agreed that in this sphere the French Revolution made next to no difference at all. The removal of economic constraints by the men of 1789 was, as Pierre Goubert puts it [40], 'permissive, not decisive'. The greatest of all these removals, the abolition of 'feudalism', is now seen to have been less final than was once thought, thanks to persistent survivals and the tendency of lords to compensate themselves for losses through higher rents. The Revolution, meanwhile, disrupted economic life and brought French overseas trade near to total destruction. Down to the 1840s the economy of France remained sluggish and unadventurous, its structure little changed since the expansive years of the mid eighteenth century. What transformed it was the advent of railways, which broke down the old regional agricultural pattern, created a national market, and gave an enormous stimulus to heavy industry with demands for coal, iron and steel [92]. This really brought the economic Ancien Regime to an end, and it happened between 1840 and 1870. Only then did agricultural productivity begin to rise above immemorial levels, towns grow to unprecedented size, and modern factory production begin to seem the industrial norm. Only then, too, did the prestige of landownership begin to fade, and the France of the monarchically-inclined *Notables* retreat before the mass forces of democratic republicanism.

These changes also had a cultural dimension. The cultural impact of the Revolution, with its onslaught on local customs and habits, its national language and imagery, and above all its attempt at dechristianisation, is unlikely ever to be underestimated. Debate over the multifarious legacies of the Revolution was to tear the country's educated elite apart for over a century. Yet when the upheaval was over, much remained as before. Catholicism was to be the religion of the vast majority of the French until the Third Republic. The steady advance in literacy was undisturbed, one way or the other, by revolutionary turmoil. The process was practically complete by the 1880s [98]. In the world of work, it was not until much the same period that the pre-industrial values, habits and attitudes of artisans and peasants began to die away [101].

In all these ways it can be argued that the deeper, non-political Ancien Regime did not really die until the second half of the nineteenth century, and that if any political revolution stood at the crossroads, and even then coincidentally, it was that of 1848 rather than 1789. Can the same be said for Europe as a whole? In one basic respect the end of the European Ancien Regime was visible from the 1730s. For it was during that decade that the relentless rise in population that is still going on began. In almost every country of Europe births began to outstrip deaths as famine and epidemics grew less frequent and human management of the environment improved. An even more modern demographic feature, mass family limitation, first appeared in France half a century later, but was not widespread throughout the continent for a further century. Economic precocity of a different sort was visible in England before the end of the eighteenth century as the industrial revolution got under way. Apart from Belgium, nothing comparable was to be seen in continental states until the 1840s, when as in France the impact of the railways proved decisive [128]. By then feudalism in the countryside, and serfdom, its most spectacular manifestation, was crumbling everywhere. A few relics survived into the twentieth century, but by the end of the 1860s the vast majority of the European peasantry were free [107]. The way was then clear, argues Jerome Blum, the historian of this emancipation, for a modern class society to replace the old society of orders. He seems uncertain, however, whether that actually happened much before 1914; and the evidence which makes him so cautious has persuaded at least one other historian that the Ancien Regime remained alive, if not entirely healthy, well into the twentieth century. Industrialisation, urbanisation and the rise of a capitalistic bourgeoisie favouring representative government certainly made spectacular progress in the course of the nineteenth century. But Arno J. Mayer argues [122] that down to 1914 agriculture was still the predominant element in the European economy, most Europeans remained country-dwellers, and most countries were still ruled by monarchs and aristocracies whose power was rooted in land and service. In this sense the Ancien Regime persisted, and its representatives were determined not to give up their power to new forces. The militarisation of Europe in the generation before 1914 reflected that determination, and the ruling orders on all sides in that year saw war as a way of saving and reinforcing their threatened authority. They miscalculated. 1914 saw the beginning of the 'Thirty Years' War of the twentieth century', and it was this struggle that finally destroyed the Ancien Regime.

Whatever they might think of this stimulating argument [132], most historians nowadays would certainly agree that the Ancien Regime did not end suddenly, but petered out over several generations. This would have saddened the men of 1789, whose intention was to shatter it with a few swift blows. And they would certainly have been appalled to think that, two hundred years after they condemned it to death, its last agonies would still be within living memory.

Select Bibliography

This bibliography makes no claims to be comprehensive. It merely lists all writings referred to in the text, along with a number of others not directly referred to but still of central importance to the study of the Ancien Regime. The bibliographies and footnotes of the works listed below are full of citations to guide interested readers towards further study.

English editions of French works are given wherever they exist.

Historians and the Ancien Regime

[1] R. Herr, *Tocqueville and the Old Regime* (1962). Fundamental to understanding the approach of the Ancien Regime's greatest historian.

[2] H. Brogan, *Tocqueville* (1973). Useful introduction.

[3] F. Furet, *Interpreting the French Revolution* (1981). Contains an important essay on Tocqueville, as well as a famous polemic against Marxist interpretations of the end of the Ancien Regime.

[4] A. Cobban, 'Hippolyte Taine, historian of the French Revolution', *History*, LIII (1968).

[5] A. Cobban, *Historians and the causes of the French Revolution* (1946). Reprinted in *Aspects of the French Revolution* (1968).

[6] J. McManners, 'The historiography of the French Revolution', in A. Goodwin (ed.), *New Cambridge Modern History*, VIII, *The American and French Revolutions 1763–93* (1965).

[7] A. Gérard, *La Révolution française: mythes et interprétations, 1789–1970* (1970).

[8] C. Mazauric, *Sur la Révolution Française* (1970). Marxist polemics in response to revisionist criticism.

[9] F. Mignet, *Histoire de la Révolution Française* (1824). Begins with the Ancien Regime from the liberal revolutionary viewpoint.

[10] F. X. J. Droz, *Histoire du Règne de Louis XVI pendant les années où l'on pouvait prévenir ou diriger la Révolution française* (1839–42), 3 vols.

[11] S. Mellon, *The political uses of history: a study of historians of the French Restoration* (New York, 1958). Sets [9] in context.

[12] P. Farmer, *France reviews its revolutionary origins. Social politics and historical opinion in the third republic* (1944).
[13] J. H. M. Salmon, 'Venality of office and popular sedition in seventeenth-century France: a review of a controversy', *Past and Present*, 37 (1967).
[14] A. Arriaza, 'Mousnier, Barber and the "society of orders"', *Past and Present*, 89 (1980).
[15] R. C. Mettam, 'Two-dimensional history: Mousnier and the Ancien Regime', *History*, LXVI (1981).
[16] J. M. Roberts, *The Mythology of the Secret Societies* (1972). Surveys some conspiracy theories of the end of the Ancien Regime.
[17] J. M. Roberts, 'The French origins of the "right"', *Transactions of the Royal Historical Society*, 5th series, 23 (1973).

The Ancien Regime in France

A. General Works

[18] A. de Tocqueville, *The Ancien Regime and the French Revolution* (1875, many editions since). The still-fruitful starting point of all study.
[19] H. Taine, *Les origines de la France contemporaine, I l'Ancien Régime* (1876; English trans., 1896). Essential for understanding much early twentieth-century writing.
[20] J. Jaurès, *Histoire socialiste de la Révolution française. I La Constituante* (1903; new edn, 1939). The founding work of the left-wing interpretation of both Ancien Regime and Revolution.
[21] A. J. M. P. Barnave, *Introduction à la Révolution française*, F. Rude (ed.) (1960). Rediscovered by Marxist historians a century after its first publication in 1843. A historical curiosity rather than an acceptable analysis.
[22] A. Cherest, *La Chute de l'Ancien Régime (1787–1789)* (1884–6), 3 vols.
[23] F. Funck-Brentano, *The Old Regime in France* (1926; Eng.trans., 1929). The least abrasive of right-wing interpretations.
[24] P. Gaxotte, *The French Revolution* (1928; Eng.trans., 1932). The most popular of right-wing interpretations; not by a scholar.
[25] M. Marion, *Dictionnaire des Institutions de la France aux XVIIe et XVIIIe siècles* (1923; reprinted 1968). A fundamental, if very biased, work of reference.
[26] P. Sagnac, *La formation de la société française moderne* (1945–6), 2 vols.
[27] H. Méthiver, *L'Ancien Régime* (1961).
[28] H. Méthiver, *Le siècle de Louis XIII* (1964).
[29] H. Méthiver, *Le siécle de Louis XIV* (1950).
[30] H. Méthiver, *Le siècle de Louis XV* (1965).
[31] H. Méthiver, *La fin de l'Ancien Régime* (1970). Highly schematic volumes. Right-wing bias. Recently (1983) republished as a single volume.

[32] R. Mousnier, *The institutions of France under the Absolute Monarchy 1598–1789* (1974 and 1980: Eng.trans., 1980 and 1983), 2 vols. Huge, sprawling, conceptually very disappointing, but full of information.

[33] A. Soboul, *La France à la veille de la Révolution. I. Economie et société* (1961). The most recent left-wing interpretation.

[34] A. Cobban, 'The myth of the French Revolution' (1955). Reprinted in *Aspects of the French Revolution* (1968). The starting point of the modern debate on the Revolution and its origins.

[35] A. Cobban, *The social interpretation of the French Revolution* (1964). The major mid-century attack on prevailing interpretations of the Revolution and its origins.

[36] C. B. A. Behrens, *The Ancien Régime* (1967). Perverse but stimulating, and well illustrated.

[37] R. Mandrou, *Introduction à la France moderne (1500–1640). Essai de psychologie historique* (1961). A pioneering approach in its time.

[38] R. Mandrou, *La France aux XVIIᵉ et XVIIIᵉ siècles* (1967). Summarises a generation's work, not always very coherently.

[39] D. Richet, *La France Moderne: l'esprit des institutions* (1973). Thoughtful essay.

[40] P. Goubert, *L'Ancien Régime I: La Société* (1962: Eng.trans., 1973). *L'Ancien Régime II: Les Pouvoirs* (1973). Far and away the best modern analysis. Subtle, humane, well-informed.

[41] P. Goubert and D. Roche, *Les Français et l'Ancien Régime* (1984), 2 vols. Illustrated and lavishly produced revision of [40].

[42] G. Cabourdin and J. Viard, *Lexique historique de la France d'Ancien Régime* (1978). Useful work of reference. More up-to-date than [25].

[43] W. Doyle, *Origins of the French Revolution* (1980). Includes bibliographical introduction.

[44] W. G. Runciman, 'Unnecessary revolution: the case of France', *Journal of European Sociology*, xxiv (1983).

B. *Political Aspects*

[45] M. Antoine, *Le conseil du Roi sous le règne de Louis XV* (1970).

[46] R. Bonney, *Political change in France under Richelieu and Mazarin 1624–1661* (1978).

[47] J. F. Bosher, '*Chambres de justice* in the French monarchy' in J. F. Bosher (ed.), *French government and society 1500–1850. Essays in memory of Alfred Cobban* (1973).

[48] J. F. Bosher, *French Finances 1770–1795. From business to bureaucracy* (1970).

[49] A. Cobban, 'The *parlements* of France in the eighteenth century'. Reprinted in *Aspects of the French Revolution* (1968).

[50] W. Doyle, 'The parlements of France and the breakdown of the old regime 1770–1788', *French Historical Studies* (1970). Interpretation opposed to [49].

[51] J. Egret, *Louis XV et l'opposition parlementaire 1715–1774* (1970).

[52] J. Flammermont, *Le chancelier Maupeou et les parlements* (1883).
[53] P. Gaxotte, *Louis XV and his times* (1934: Eng.trans., 1934).
[54] E. Glasson, *Le parlement de Paris. Son role politique depuis le règne de Charles VII jusqu'à la Révolution* (1901), 2 vols.
[55] A. N. Hamscher, *The Parlement of Paris after the Fronde* (1976).
[56] J. M. Hayden, *France and the Estates General of 1614* (1974).
[57] L. Laugier, *Un ministère réformateur sous Louis XV. Le triumvirat* (1975). Strong right-wing bias.
[58] P. S. Lewis, 'The failure of the French medieval estates', *Past and Present*, 23 (1962).
[59] J. Russell Major, *Representative government in early modern France* (1980).
[60] R. Mousnier, *La vénalité des offices sous Henri IV et Louis XIII* (2nd edn, 1971). Mousnier's most important work. Will outlast the others.
[61] R. Mousnier, *Le conseil du roi de Louis XII à la Révolution* (1970). Collected essays.
[62] R. Mousnier, *La plume, la faucille et le marteau* (1970). Collected essays.
[63] F. Olivier-Martin, *L'organisation corporative de la France sous l'Ancien Régime* (1938).
[64] G. Pagès, *La monarchie d'Ancien Régime en France* (1928). Founding work in modern study of the Ancien Regime monarchy.
[65] D. Parker, *The making of French Absolutism* (1983). A useful up-to-date survey. Good on medieval origins.
[66] B. Pocquet, *Le duc d'Aiguillon et La Chalotais* (1900), 3 vols.
[67] D. Richet, 'Autour des origines idéologiques lointaines de la Révolution: élites et despotisme', *Annales ESC* (1967). A seminal article in the evolution of the idea of the *Notables*.
[68] J. H. Shennan, *The parlement of Paris* (1968).
[69] G. V. Taylor, 'Revolutionary and non-revolutionary content in the *cahiers* of 1789. An interim report', *French Historical Studies* (1973).

C. Social Aspects

[70] B. Behrens, 'Nobles, privileges and taxes in France at the end of the Ancien Regime', *Econ HR*, XV (1962–3). Important early revisionism in English.
[71] G. Chaussinand-Nogaret, *Une histoire des élites, 1700–1848* (1975).
[72] G. Chaussinand-Nogaret, *The French Nobility in the eighteenth century. From Feudalism to Enlightenment* (1976: Eng.trans., 1985).
[73] E. Coornaert, *Les corporations en France avant 1789* (1941).
[74] W. Doyle, 'The price of offices in eighteenth century France', *Historical Journal* (1984).
[75] G. Duby, *The three orders: feudal society imagined* (1979: Eng.trans., 1980).
[76] G. Ellis, 'Rhine and Loire: Napoleonic elites and social order', in G. Lewis and C. Lucas (eds), *Beyond the Terror. Essays in French Regional and Social History, 1794–1815* (1983).
[77] F. L. Ford, *Robe and Sword. The regrouping of the French Aristocracy after Louis XIV* (1953).

[78] R. Forster, 'The French Revolution and the "new" elite, 1800–50', in J. Pelenski (ed.), *The American and European Revolutions 1776–1848* (1980).
[79] C. Loyseau, *Cinq livres du droit des offices, suivis du livre des seigneuries et de celui des Ordres* (1610). Seventeenth-century treatise heavily relied upon by Mousnier.
[80] C. Lucas, 'Nobles, bourgeois, and the origins of the French Revolution', *Past and Present* (1973). Reprinted in D. Johnson (ed.), *French Society and the Revolution* (1976).
[81] R. Mousnier, *Social Hierarchies* (1969: Eng.trans., London 1973).
[82] R. Mousnier, 'Recherches sur les soulèvements populaires en France avant la Fronde', *Revue d'histoire moderne et contemporaine*, IV (1958).
[83] R. Mousnier, *Peasant uprisings in seventeenth century France, Russia and China* (1967: Eng.trans., 1971).
[84] G. Pagès, 'La vénalité des offices dans l'ancienne France', *Revue Historique*, CLXIX (1932).
[85] B. Porchnev, *Les soulèvements populaires de 1623 à 1648* (1963).

D. *Economic Aspects*

[86] J. Dupâquier, *La population française aux XVIIe et XVIIIe siècles* (1979). Convenient summary of latest research.
[87] C.E. Labrousse, *Esquisse du mouvement des prix et des revenus en France au XVIIIe siècle* (1933) 2 vols.
[88] C.E. Labrousse, *La crise de l'économie française à la fin de l'Ancien Régime* (1944). Two founding works for all modern study.
[89] E. LeRoy Ladurie, 'History that stands still', in *The mind and method of the historian* (1981). Attack on [91].
[90] H. Lüthy, *La Banque Protestante en France de la révocation de l'Edit de Nantes à la Révolution* (1959), 2 vols.
[91] M. Morineau, *Les faux-semblants d'un démarrage économique. Agriculture et démographie en France au XVIIIe siècle* (1971). A challenging interpretation. Controversial. Attacked by [89].
[92] R. Price, *An economic history of modern France 1730–1914* (1981).
[93] F. Simiand, *Recherches anciennes et nouvelles sur le mouvement général des prix du XVIe au XIXe siècle* (1932).
[94] G.V. Taylor, 'Types of capitalism in eighteenth century France', *EHR* (1964).
[95] G.V. Taylor, 'Noncapitalist wealth and the origins of the French Revolution', *American HR*, LXXII (1967). Most influential article in the debate on the Revolution's origins.

E. *Cultural Aspects*

[96] R. Darnton, 'The high Enlightenment and the low life of literature in pre-revolutionary France', *Past and Present*, 51 (1971).
[97] R. Darnton, *The business of Enlightenment. A publishing history of the Encyclopédie 1775–1800* (1979).

[98] F. Furet and J. Ozouf, *Reading and writing. Literacy in France from Calvin to Jules Ferry* (1977, Eng.trans., 1982).

[99] N. Hampson, *Will and Circumstance. Montesquieu, Rousseau and the French Revolution* (1983).

[100] J. Quéniart, *Les hommes, l'église et dieu dans la France du XVIIIe siècle* (1978).

[101] W.M. Reddy, *The rise of market culture. The textile trade and French Society 1750–1900* (1984). Brilliant thesis on the outlook of Ancien Regime workers, and its persistence.

[102] D. Roche, *Le siècle des lumières en Province. Académies et académiciens provinciaux 1680–1789* (1978), 2 vols.

[103] M. Vovelle, *Piété baroque et déchristianisation en Provence au XVIIIe siècle* (1973).

The Ancien Regime Beyond France

[104] P. Anderson, *Passages from Antiquity to Feudalism* (1974). The first part of a brilliant but controversial Marxist reinterpretation of the sweep of modern European history.

[105] P. Anderson, *Lineages of the Absolutist State* (1974). Second part of [104].

[106] M. Beloff, *The Age of Absolutism 1660–1815* (1954).

[107] J. Blum, *The End of the Old Order in Rural Europe* (1978).

[108] F. Braudel, *The Mediterranean and the Mediterranean world in the Age of Philip 11* (1949: Eng.trans., 1973), 2 vols. One of the most important works of history of this century. Teems with ideas for confronting the issues posed by the Ancien Regime.

[109] F. Braudel, *Civilisation and Capitalism 15th–18th century* (1979: Eng. trans., 1981–4):
  (1) *The Structures of Everyday Life* (1981);
  (2) *The Wheels of Commerce* (1982);
  (3) *The Perspective of the World* (1984).
  Braudel's testament. Exciting and brilliantly stimulating. The best introduction to early modern economic history.

[110] R. Brenner, 'Agrarian class structure and economic development in pre-industrial Europe', *Past and Present*, 70 (1976) and

[111] Symposium, *Past and Present*, 97 (1982).

[112] P. Burke, *Popular culture in early modern Europe* (1978). Pioneering survey.

[113] A. Corvisier, *Armies and society in Europe from 1494 to 1789* (1976: Eng.trans., 1979).

[114] R. Davis, *The rise of the Atlantic Economies* (1973).

[115] J. Delumeau, *Catholicism between Luther and Voltaire: a new view of the Counter-Reformation* (1971: Eng.trans., 1977). Excellent summary of recent work, with extensive bibliography.

[116] W. Doyle, *The Old European Order 1660–1800* (1978).

[117] M. W. Flinn, *The European demographic system 1500–1820* (1981).

[118] D. Gerhard, *Old Europe. A study in continuity 1000–1800* (1981).

[119] H. Kamen, *European Society 1500–1700* (1984).

[120] P. Laslett, *The World we have lost* (1965, 3rd edn, 1983).

[121] R. Mandrou, *L'Europe 'absolutiste' 1649–1775* (1977, New edn 1980 entitled *La Raison du Prince*).

[122] A. J. Mayer, *The persistence of the Old Regime. Europe to the great War* (1981). The most controversial recent treatment of the end of the Ancien Regime.

[123] J. Meyer, *Noblesses et pouvoirs dans l'Europe d'Ancien Regime* (1973).

[124] R. R. Palmer, *The Age of the Democratic Revolution* (1) *The Challenge* (1959).

[125] L. Réau, *L'Europe française au siècle des lumières* (1951).

[126] M. Roberts, 'The military revolution, 1560–1660', in *Essays in Swedish History* (1967).

[127] A. Sorel, *Europe and the French Revolution* (1885: Eng.trans., vol 1, ed. A. Cobban and J. W. Hunt, 1969).

[128] C. Trebilcock, *The industrialisation of the continental powers* (1981).

[129] I. Wallerstein, *The modern world-system* (1974-80), 2 vols. Dazzling synthesis of early modern economic history. Deep influence on [109].

[130] E. N. Williams, *The Ancien Regime in Europe. Government and Society in the major states 1648–1789* (1970).

[131] M. Raeff, *The well-ordered police state: social and institutional change through the law in the Germanies and Russia 1600–1800* (1983).

[132] G. Eley and D. Blackbourn (eds), *The Peculiarities of German History : bourgeois society and politics in nineteenth century Germany* (1984). Raises important doubts about [122].

[133] C. B. A. Behrens, *Society, Government and the Enlightenment. The experiences of eighteenth century France and Prussia* (1985). Useful and unusual comparisons.

Index